Reconciliation and Transformation

Reconciliation *and* Transformation

Reconsidering Christian Theologies of the Cross

Jesper Svartvik

TRANSLATED BY
Karen Hagersten

CASCADE *Books* • Eugene, Oregon

RECONCILIATION AND TRANSFORMATION
Reconsidering Christian Theologies of the Cross

First published in Sweden by Verbum Förlag AB, Stockholm

Cascade Books
An Imprint of Wipf and Stock Publishers
199 W. 8th Ave., Suite 3
Eugene, OR 97401

www.wipfandstock.com

PAPERBACK ISBN: 978-1-6667-0760-1
HARDCOVER ISBN: 978-1-6667-0761-8
EBOOK ISBN: 978-1-6667-0762-5

Cataloguing-in-Publication data:

Names: Svartvik, Jesper, author. | Hagersten, Karen, translator.

Title: Reconciliation and transformation : reconsidering Christian theologies of the cross / by Jesper Svartvik : translated by Karen Hagersten.

Description: Eugene, OR: Cascade Books, 2021 | Includes bibliographical references and index.

Identifiers: ISBN 978-1-6667-0760-1 (paperback) | ISBN 978-1-6667-0761-8 (hardcover) | ISBN 978-1-6667-0762-5 (ebook)

Subjects: LCSH: Salvation | Reconciliation—Religious aspects—Christianity | Deification (Christianity)—History of doctrines | Theology of the Cross | Atonement

Classification: BT751.2 S837 2021 (print) | BT751.2 (ebook)

08/18/21

Contents

Preface

THE NEED FOR RECONCILIATION and the significance of renewal are two of the most fundamental aspects of a person's life. These concepts are essential to Christian faith. Many would claim they are the very core of the Christian religion and lifeblood of their Christian faith.

The concepts may be fundamental, yet they remain vague to many people. Nothing in Christian theology is more inevitable than Christology, that is, what Christians say about Jesus of Nazareth. In Christology, nothing may be more difficult to grasp than the interpretations of the accounts of Jesus' death on the cross. Furthermore, no aspect of his suffering and death is more difficult to explain than the assertion that it should have something to do with reconciliation.

The concept of *reconciliation* has been discussed more extensively in the Western Christian tradition than in the Eastern Church, where instead weight is placed on deification (in Greek *theōsis*), which in this book has been called *transformation*. These two words, reconciliation and transformation, express a desire to combine Christianity's Western and Eastern traditions. The task of this book is to contribute to some extent to a deeper knowledge and understanding of reconciliation and transformation, what they are and mean to us.

Jesper Svartvik

Acknowledgments

THIS BOOK IS AN independent continuation of the book *Förundran och förväntan* (Amazement and Anticipation). The first and last chapters of that book are especially devoted to creation theology (including the wonder many experience living in and beholding our world) and eschatology (that is, the expectations that many people express faced with the challenges and promises of the future). The longest section of the book is, however, the fifth chapter, which is about reconciliation. Many readers have contacted me and told me that that specific chapter has been especially valuable for them in processing and discussing various aspects of the Christian faith. This book delves more deeply into the issues presented in the previous book's chapter on the theological interpretations of the death of Jesus.

For valuable and appreciated comments on early drafts of this text I wish to extend a heartfelt thanks to Mats Ekström, Jan Hermanson, Göran Larsson, Svante Lundgren, Inger Nebel, Jakob Wirén, and Sara Yarden. For stimulating discussions and letters on the subjects that were treated in this book I also wish to thank Raymond Cohen, Helene Egnell, Reuven Kipperwasser, Liv Ingeborg Lied, Anna Frydenberg, Julie Pelc Adler, and Abraham Zvi Schwarcz (*Shav-Aretz*). An initial version of chapter seven was published in *Making a Difference: Essays on the Bible and Judaism in Honor of Tamara Cohn Eskenazi* in 2012. I am grateful to David J. A. Clines at Sheffield Phoenix Press for granting permission to publish a revised version of the article in this book. It has been a pleasure to work with Karen Hagersten, who has translated the Swedish original into English, and with Lotten Wesslén, who has assisted me editing the manuscript.

After ten years of teaching and research in Jerusalem, I am currently serving as the Corcoran Visiting Chair at Boston College. I would like to express my deep gratitude for both stimulating cooperation and conversations with my colleagues, especially Ruth Langer and Camille Fitzpatrick Markey, with whom I work at the Center for Christian-Jewish Learning. It is a distinct honor to serve at one of the leading universities in the field of theology, divinity, and religious studies.

It is a great pleasure and privilege for me to dedicate this book to Tamara Cohn Eskenazi, Professor of Biblical Literature and History at Hebrew Union College in Los Angeles. She is a prominent scholar, an appreciated educator, and a close friend. We first met in Ariccia, near Rome, at a conference that resulted in the book *Christ Jesus and the Jewish People Today* in October 2006. Since then, we have met annually at the conferences of the Society of Biblical Literature and discussed the issues touched upon in this book. No presentation at an international conference with thousands of participants can be compared with a conversation over breakfast with Tamara *panim el-panim* ("face-to-face"). *Ha-sepher ha-zeh muqdash lakh be-hoqarah.*

1
Introduction

EVERY HUMAN BEING IS likely to experience moments of despair, need forgiveness, or long for reconciliation and redemption. The dread of not performing well enough, of not sufficing in the eyes of others, of not being worthy afflicts many of us. The questions of sin and shame are universal and therefore shared, though some Christians have taken pains to express them more often than others. This book is about the internal scars we bear in silence.

The message of the forgiveness of sins is one of the dominant motifs in the history of Christian thought, especially in Reformed theology, and perhaps particularly in the Lutheran tradition. It can be described as the theological crown jewel and the most sacred of the sacrosanct in Christianity. "The church is a community constituted by the forgiveness of sins," writes Haddon Willmer.[1] This line of thought is perhaps most famously and exactingly expressed by Karl Barth when he writes, "There never was and there never can be any true Christian church without the doctrine of justification. In this sense it is indeed *articulus stantis et cadentis ecclesiae* [the article of belief by which the church stands or falls]."[2]

The need for reconciliation, what Barth calls justification, and the importance of renewal are thus crucial tenets of Christian doctrine. Many

1. Willmer, "Forgiveness," 246. For critical viewpoints of the claim that Paul's main—or, indeed, his *only*—mission was the forgiveness of sins, see Stendahl, *Paul*, 1–96. Stendahl argues that Paul should instead be understood as an apostle of the gentiles who was convinced that the peoples (that is, non-Jews) would be included in the commonwealth of the God of Israel. For a presentation of the scholarly legacy of Stendahl, see Fredriksen & Svartvik, eds., *Krister*.

2. Barth, *Church Dogmatics*, IV.1.523. The expression, *articulus stantis et cadentis ecclesiae* (or, the more correct version, *articulus stantis vel cadentis ecclesiae*) has been used by Reformed theologians since the 1600s; e.g., Mahlmann, " Rechtfertigung," *Zur Rechtfertigungslehre*, 167–271.

people, and not least those of the Lutheran tradition, would probably even be prepared to say it is the very core of the Christian faith. Seeking new perspectives and ways to express them might therefore be seen at first glance as questioning, which can evoke strong reactions. As these are more or less unavoidable questions, it is important to raise them respectfully, in part because they are about something deeply *human,* and in part because they are ultimately about a *mystery,* something we can never truly understand, merely anticipate. Fragile and vulnerable though we are, we struggle to grasp these great questions that are so important to us.

A Faith That Seeks Understanding

In *Amazement and Anticipation* I emphasize the importance of differentiating between the Swedish words *betvivla* and *förtvivla* (approximately, questioning and despairing).[3] This applies especially when we speak of reconciliation and renewal. What is one to believe? May a believer doubt? Just as there are different kinds of faith, we can naturally speak of different kinds of doubt. Believers have always questioned and sought answers, which has involved posing critical questions about faith. Anselm of Canterbury (1033–1109) defined theology as "faith seeking understanding" (Latin *fides quaerens intellectum*).[4] Therefore, it is actually impossible to believe if no questions are posed and no answers sought. The book of Ecclesiastes, observes Hubert J. Richards, would probably never have been included in the Bible if it were considered wrong by definition to ask critical questions:

> Why did they not they condemn Ecclesiastes as a heretic for daring to criticize the answers people had given in the past to human misery? Perhaps because they saw that his questioning faith was more worthwhile than the faith which never asks questions. After all, who is the true believer, the man who simply repeats the answers his forefathers have handed on to him because they comfort him, or this "disbeliever" who broke through to the realization that we have to put our faith not in answers, but in God[?][5]

3. Svartvik, *Förundran*, 47–52.

4. See *Proslogion*, 2–4. See also Plantinga, Thompson, and Lundberg, *Introduction*, 8.

5. Richards, *Death and After*, 126. One of the key concepts in Ecclesiastes, *havel havalim* (1:2), is often translated to "vanity of vanities" or "futility of futilities." The word *hevel* is related to puff of wind and breath. The human breath is a manifestation of life itself and its fragility. Abel's name in Hebrew is *Hevel* (Gen 4). He lived neither a vain nor a void life, but a *short* one, murdered by his brother, Cain. Perhaps the message intended in

One of the goals of this book is to review critically and question some of the statements that are often made about the background to and consequences of Jesus' death; there is good reason to wonder if they are correct and true in all regards.

Salvation or Reconciliation?

What is actually meant by the words salvation, reconciliation (or justification), and redemption? They more or less overlap, but they are not identical, and should therefore not be used as synonyms. The Swedish verb *frälsa* comes from the word *frihalsa,* which referred to the physical action of releasing a slave from a slave collar.[6] The Greek word *sōtēria* and the Hebrew word *geulah* can also be translated as "salvation" (if used in a religious context) or "rescue" (if a physical action is intended).[7] David F. Ford reminds us that the English word "salvation" comes from *salus,* the Latin word for "health." Health can be spiritual, social, political, financial, environmental, mental, or moral. If salvation has to do with God the creator, we cannot disregard any of these dimensions.[8] Ford also refers to what he calls "the three main dynamics of Christian living," namely (a) *worship and prayer;* (b) *living and learning in community;* and (c) *speech, action, and suffering for justice, freedom, peace, goodness, and truth.*[9] At times, Christian discussion may well have been limited to the first dynamic, but now, as we seek a more holistic perspective, how can it be related to all three dynamics?

In this book, however, the term *reconciliation* will primarily be used, rather than salvation. There are three reasons for this choice: (a) Firstly,

---

Ecclesiastes was not one of futility or emptiness but that nothing in this world is permanent. Meir Zlotowitz and Nosson Scherman liken *hevel* to fireworks; see *Koheles*, xxxviii: "The colors and design are dazzling, breathtaking. But in a matter of moments, they are gone." The word *hevel* occurs about as often as does *Elohim* (God) in Ecclesiastes; might one of the messages of the book be that humans and all else passes, only God remains? If so, perhaps the message would be better translated to "the most transient."

6. Wessén, *Våra ord, s.v.*

7. A number of words related to salvation can be traced to the root *y-sh-'*, more specifically, *yeshu'ah*, translated in the Septuagint as *sōtēria*. For a comparative study of the concept and phenomenon of salvation in a number of religious traditions, see Werblowsky & Bleeker, eds., *Types of Redemption*.

8. Ford, *Self and Salvation*, 1.

9. Ford, *Self and Salvation*, 5: "worship and prayer; living and learning in community; and speech, action and suffering for justice, freedom, peace, goodness and truth."

the concept of salvation sometimes carries *an escapist content.* It was not unavoidable that the word should come to be understood in this way, but unfortunately it has. Often it involves evading rather than receiving. Rather than attempt a rehabilitation of the word salvation, might we not find other words that correspond better to what we want to discuss?[10]

(b) Secondly, there has been *a self-centering tendency* in the use of the word salvation. The concept of reconciliation, on the other hand, comprises (at least) two parties. Reconciliation can take place between two states, nations, individuals, or, theologically, between God and humanity.[11] Raymond Cohen, an international relations scholar, writes that negotiation between two parties presupposes a certain level of trust between them. Reconciliation, trust, and negotiation have much in common.[12]

(c) Thirdly, it is possible to speak of a reconciliation process—to clarify that it is a matter of *a development that is taxing of both one's time and strength,* whereas the concept of a "salvation process" is not as common. One might ask the question, what characterizes a reconciliation process? Or, more concretely, what are the prerequisites for genuine reconciliation to take place? In the ninth chapter, "Transformation," the task of cultivating a culture of reconciliation will be discussed. As we shall see, there is a connection between reconciliation and redemption.

A fundamental intent of this book is that *the concept of reconciliation in Christian theology should not diverge from the way it is used in the Bible.* Before addressing Christian theories of reconciliation, we need to become familiar with the main questions of New Testament atonement theology. And in order to gain a deeper understanding of the New Testament authors' mission, we must first get to know the Old Testament writings, that is, the Hebrew Bible.[13] *The emphasis in this book will be on understanding*

10. Cf. Lossky, *Mystical Theology*, 135: "*salvation.* This negative term stands for the removal of an obstacle: one is saved from something—from death, and from sin—its root." See also Camnerin and Fritzon, *Försoning behövs*, 17–19.

11. We can also use the term reconciliation to describe the process of reconciling with oneself. In each case, two dynamics must meet. On one side there is often a distressing situation, and on the other side is the insight that there must be some way to manage the situation.

12. See Cohen, *Negotiating across Cultures*, 225–26.

13. Thus, even the concept of reconciliation has its burdens and limitations. Three major motifs of reconciliation in Christian theology are usually presented in textbooks and scholarly summaries: (a) the *objective* (or, the *Latin*) model of reconciliation developed by Anselm of Canterbury and in Reformed theology, (b) Pierre Abélard's *subjective* model, and (c) Gustaf Aulén's dramatic model—which he called the *classic*

the concept of reconciliation in relation to the worship services at the temple of Jerusalem during the time of Jesus. This book will specifically address the assumption that, in the Bible, holy violence is a prerequisite of reconciliation. This book also pays special attention to the temple metaphor because the first Christians were Jews, and the temple of Jerusalem still existed. Yet, only a few generations later, Christianity had become primarily a *non*-Jewish movement, and the temple had been destroyed. In what way did these *historical* phenomena influence the *theological* development of the concept of reconciliation?

In the Shadow of the Cross

The cross is both the central symbol of Christianity and an indispensable aspect of the identity of countless Christians the world over.[14] The cross is a symbol that gives strength, courage, and perseverance. In no way should this book make light of this piety toward the cross. Indeed, it may be that only those who see and realize the meaning of the cross and its inherent strength as a symbol can think both critically and constructively about these questions.

In Jaroslav Pelikan's book, *Jesus through the Centuries,* each chapter is illustrated and summarized by a cross. As a result, nineteen different crosses inscribe the nineteen chapters, factually illustrating two aspects of Christian theology: first, there are different ways to interpret and apply the life and teachings of Jesus, and second, all of them, in one way or another, have to do with his crucifixion. The cross is the most known symbol of and in Christianity.

Yet many people are disturbed by the cross. In the words of Swedish writer Carl Johan Wallgren, "This bloody, suffering God frightens away people. Why have we not been able to find a more beautiful symbol for our

model—with emphasis on *Christus Victor* (Christ the Victor). For a presentation of these three models, see Aulén's influential book, *Christus Victor*. The fifth chapter of this book analyzes the concept of violence being a necessary condition for reconciliation. In fact, the violence metaphor is striking in all three models. Anselm undoubtedly sanctions violence, Abélard appears to romanticize suffering, and even Aulén's emphasis on the struggle motif can be seen as resulting in an overemphasis on violence as a metaphor and condition. Aulén does discuss the motif of deification, but the violence metaphor weighs more heavily in his presentation than does *theōsis*.

14. It is not uncommon for Coptic Christians to tattoo a cross on, for example, their right wrist or arm (cf. Ps 137:5).

faith?"[15] In a world of so much suffering and death, many ask why Christian churches, Christian art, and Christian preaching must emphasize Jesus' suffering and death. And if Jesus' violent death is not only unavoidable but is also a form of deliverance, does it not mean that violence in our own time is also a form of deliverance? If so, in what way? If not, why was violence a form of deliverance then and there but not here and now?

Clearly, there are many pressing questions to ask, and we will explore them in turn. First of all, we need to analyze carefully what is probably the most widespread of all the interpretations of Jesus' suffering and death. We will do that in the next chapter.

15. Vallgren, *Den vidunderliga kärleken*, 123.

2

Preunderstandings of the Cross Event

SCHOLARS OF *HERMENEUTICS*, OR the study of interpretation, sometimes use the concept of *preunderstanding* to describe the unavoidable fact that our interpretations are never unconditional, because they come to us prepackaged in an interpretational framework that greatly influences us when we interpret a phenomenon or a text.[1] We do not read a telephone catalog, for example, in the way we read a poem, nor do we read a letter from the tax authorities as we would read a love letter. If a text begins with the words, "Once upon a time," our thoughts are led in a direction very different from if it had begun with the words "Take three eggs and mix them with . . . ." In other words, we have completely different expectations of different types of texts, and these expectations direct our interpretations.

The question, then, is what preunderstanding might affect our conceptions of reconciliation in Christian theology. Whether or not we are aware of it, we all carry baggage packed collectively over the centuries. No one approaches theological texts without that baggage, least of all the texts that are often cited in discussions of Christian reconciliation theology. Only after we have understood this and become familiar with what we carry in our knapsack—personal experiences, social values, and theological traditions—can we appreciate the breadth of our preunderstanding, because it is a position we take subconsciously.

1. Hermeneutics comes from the Greek, *hermēneuein,* "to interpret" and *hermēneia,* "interpretation." In Greek mythology, Hermes was the messenger of the gods; see, for example, Acts 14:12: "Barnabas they called Zeus, and Paul they called Hermes, because he was the chief speaker." For a definition, see Thiselton, *Hermeneutics,* 1: "Hermeneutics explore how we read, understand, and handle texts, especially those written in another time or in a context of life different from our own. Biblical hermeneutics investigates more specifically how we read, understand, apply, and respond to biblical texts."

Traditional Atonement Theology

Clearly, there is a striking abundance of interpretations within reconciliation theology. Nonetheless, might it be possible to trace the outlines of a conventional understanding in Western Christianity, especially Protestantism, one that could even be said to be taken for granted in many settings?[2] Generalizing is always tinged with peril, and this case is no exception, yet it may be worth our while to attempt it. A review of Bible texts will demonstrate that the customary approach is far from obvious. Rather, there are many critical questions to ask about what *many Christians believe,* and what *many people believe that Christians believe,* and what *many people believe Christians are required to believe.*[3] The following description contains several citations from the Bible. These scriptures need not be interpreted in this way. It simply demonstrates how they are often interpreted. The examples show, in other words, not how these Bible citations *should be* used but rather how they *tend to be* used.

The most common interpretation of Jesus' death in Western theology can be described as a combination of language and images taken from two separate worlds: the temple and the court of law.[4] According to this interpretation, God created a world that was good ("And God saw that it was good"), yet the very first humans sinned against the word of God,[5] as do all human beings thereafter.[6] In the Augustinian tradition, named after church father Aurelius Augustinus (354–430), this is known as "original sin" (Latin *peccatum originale*), meaning that humans are said to inherit their sinful

2. Eastern Orthodox theologies, however, have emphasized *transformation* (or deification, in Greek *theōsis*) over *reconciliation.* In other words, the emphasis in those theologies has been more on the transfiguration, resurrection, and ascension of Jesus than on the events of Good Friday.

3. It is often observed, in this context, that there has never been a single theological interpretation of Jesus' crucifixion that has been acknowledged as the *correct* Christian interpretation. That is, there have always been *several* interpretations of how Christians might understand Jesus' death and the consequences of it. See, for example, Svartvik, *Textens tilltal,* 183–90.

4. See Guroian, *Melody,* 50: "The New Testament writers freely mixed and blended legal and sacerdotal metaphors because they understood that neither kind of metaphor completely captures the full mystery of salvation."

5. See Gen 1:10. To read about the offenses of Adam and Eve, see Gen 3.

6. Cf. Rom 5:12: "Therefore, just as sin came into the world through one man, and death came through sin, and so death spread to all because all have sinned." Cf. Rom 3:23: "Since all have sinned and fall short of the glory of God." For a comprehensive presentation of interpretations of 5:12, see Cranfield, *Epistle to the Romans,* 1.269–81.

nature because they are born to a world in which sin reigns. Humankind is therefore a "condemned mass" (Latin *massa damnata*). Any individual human being, already before sinning, deserves damnation. There is nothing any human can do to escape condemnation.[7] A righteous God demands justice. A holy God must be allowed to express holy wrath at the combined sin of humanity and the individual sins of humans.[8] Humans can therefore not escape damnation. Every human—adult or newborn, man or woman, incurable sinner or do-gooder—is condemned to death because every human, without exception, has violated the holy word of God.[9]

What is to be done, then, in this situation? Is there anything at all that can save humanity? At this point in this line of thinking it is often asserted that the offerings made in the Hebrew Bible were insufficient, as they were limited to a "period of respite."[10] The role thus assigned the Hebrew Bible texts puts them in the position of serving as a paradigm for a faulty piety. It is often emphasized that blood must be shed; for without blood there can be no forgiveness.[11] That is why the offerings in the temple in Jerusalem were animal offerings. This mode of thought thus reinforces the inevitable failure of humanity. The fact is that human sin is so great that every single human being deserves to die. Therefore, there must be compensation by death. In this genuinely hopeless situation, something wondrous happens: When Jesus of Nazareth dies on the cross, he takes upon himself the punishment that is actually intended for human beings. Jesus is condemned to death in the place of all human beings; he dies for humanity. When Jesus dies, God's anger is averted. God and humanity are

7. Saint Augustine, *City of God, Vol. VII, Books XXI–XXII,* trans. William M. Green: "Hence the whole mass of mankind was condemned, since he who first sinned was punished along with the stock that had its root in him, and from that just and merited punishment no one is freed except by merciful and unmerited grace." For more views on the Augustinian doctrine of sin, see Fredriksen, *Sin*, 112–34, and Belousek, *Atonement*, 365 n.10. For a comprehensive discussion of the relevance of the doctrine of original sin today, see Grantén, *Utanför paradiset*. She argues that the doctrine of original sin is not an explanation but rather an interpretation of what it means (215) "to live outside paradise" (translated, italics in original).

8. Belousek notes that it is common for Christians to be convinced that God should primarily be seen as angry; see *Atonement*, 402.

9. Cf. Rom 6:23: "For the wages of sin is death."

10. On the concept forbearance, see Rom 3:26.

11. Cf. Heb 9:22. Compare this with the rabbinical expression *ein kapparah ella bedam* (literally, "without the shedding of blood there is no forgiveness of sins") which does not provide the larger picture of Jewish and Christian reconciliation theologies.

finally reconciled. A barrier between Jews and non-Jews is abolished *post Christum* (Latin for after Christ).[12]

The Christian Cross and the Other Believers in God

According to this traditional model of reconciliation, however, one must be a Christian to be included. Just as we are being reminded that the barrier separating Jews and non-Jews has been abolished, a new line of division is established, namely that between Christians and non-Christians. For non-Christians, God remains a wrathful God. No one may come to God without Christian belief, no one may come to the Father except through the Son. Thus, it is the task of Christians to make disciples of all the peoples, that they may take part in the promise that only Christians may receive: a vital and meaningful divine relationship with a reconciled God.[13] Christianity's universal aims are cited so often that we should take a moment to remember that the early Christian community in fact represented a new, separate movement. Considering how few of them there were, we can speak of it as an exclusive group. Paul did write in one of his letters, or epistles, that "you are all one in Jesus Christ," but that referred only to those included in the Christian community.[14] The one who is not "in Christ" remains on the outside.[15]

Christian theology has faced a specific problem: The majority of Jews choose to continue living a Jewish life. Do they not see that Christians consider the barrier between Jews and non-Jews to be abolished? Should not all Jews become Christians? Living a Jewish life becomes, according to this way of thinking, a theological rebellion against God's plan. So circumcision, celebrating the Sabbath, and dietary rules, for example, become acts expressing that there are people who have not yet understood that it is not about obeying laws but rather about receiving in faith that which God granted humans in Christ, namely, the forgiveness of sins, because Christ is the end of Jewish law.[16] Jewish *halakhah* (regulations about how a Jewish

12. Cf. Eph 2:14–15. For an account of various interpretations of this passage, see the sixth chapter of this book.

13. Cf. John 14:6 and Matt 28:19–20.

14. Cf. Gal 3:28.

15. It appears that the early Christians self-identified as *tertium genus* (a third people; that is, neither Jews nor gentiles). For more views on the subject, see Svartvik, "Contemporary."

16. Cf. Rom 10:4.

life can and should be configured) is therefore for many Christians more theologically provocative than the Islamic *shari'ah* (regulations about how a Muslim life can and should be configured) because Jewish tradition is older than the Christian movement.[17] The *intra*-Jewish discussion of the application of the commandments that we find in some New Testament texts are often interpreted as *anti*-Jewish polemics. Using the sacred sanctuary of a church to regularly criticize fasting during Ramadan or Muslim prayer five times a day would surely be seen by many Christians, and correctly so, as an expression of inappropriate Islamophobia. Why should Christians speak disparagingly of another faith? Yet preaching disparagingly from a pulpit during a Christian service about, for example, the Jewish Sabbath and dietary restrictions, is not considered to be as sensational, because it is a behavior that has a history of two thousand years.

John Dominic Crossan once asked a highly relevant question: "Why . . . did Christianity arrive *and* Judaism survive?"[18] The two traditional responses are insufficient. It is not acceptable to contend that Judaism is merely the crumbling theological remains from the time of the Second Temple in Jerusalem that should no longer exist; nor is it acceptable to ignore or reject the question as theologically insignificant. Thus, Christian reconciliation theologies are significantly bound to Jewish-Christian relations, giving us good reason to revisit these questions later in the book.

The atonement model described above is problematic; it overemphasizes the crime-and-punishment dimension to the extent that it prevails. In the words of Colin E. Gunton,

> There is no doubt that there is much wrong with the Western tradition's preoccupation with the penal aspects of the atonement.[19]

What Gunton is saying is that those who see and describe Jesus primarily as a sacrifice for divine, punishing justice, which in this chapter has

17. An influential presentation of *halakhah* and *aggadah* is made by Bialik, *Halachah and Aggadah*. For a summary of the book, see his article "Law and Legend."

18. Crossan, "What Victory," 356.

19. Gunton, *Actuality of Atonement*, 15. See, as well, his important observations: "Yet the whole affair does sometimes appear to be an exercise of power rather than love, . . . the often-noted weakness that Anselm appears to equate salvation with the remission of penalty" (ibid., 93). A considerably harsher view of this reconciliation theology was expressed by Crossan, "Hymn to a Savage God," 27: "I do not believe in a God who *could* forgive gratuitously but actually does so only after Jesus has been beaten to a bloody pulp in our place. If I accepted, as I do not, this film's vision of a savage God, I hope I would have the courage to follow Mrs. Job's advice: 'Curse God, and die' (Job 2.9)."

been described as the preunderstanding many people have of Christian cross theology, are actually committing several errors. If theology uses *solely* the language of the courts ("guilty," "judgment," "punishment," "acquitted," etc.), these metaphors become isolated from others to the extent of being literally interpreted. The symbolism ceases to be symbolic. In addition, it creates a division between the ways in which God and Jesus behaved that is problematic for a Christian theology that intends to emphasize their unity and uniformity.[20]

Four Critical Questions

The reconciliation theology that has been outlined in this chapter is thus deeply problematic. There are at least four reasons for this.

(a) We have observed that the suffering and death of Jesus is likened to that of the sacrifices in the temple in Jerusalem. We must therefore be familiar with sacrifice theology in order to understand the context. In the Hebrew Bible there are several words for "sacrifice." The most general one is *qorban,* which etymologically means "to approach" or "to be near."[21] Different types of sacrifice are described in Hebrew Bible texts, but those that are best known are undeniably the animal sacrifices. We have to remember that, in biblical times, making an animal sacrifice was a way to approach the divine. *Animal sacrifice, however, is not the way we approach God in our time.*[22] There is therefore an overriding risk that we approach the texts about sacrifice with anachronistic conceptions and frameworks. Instead, we need to try to understand the sacrificial culture and sacrificial theology of those times, even if we are not necessarily attracted by them or want to adopt them. We need to remember that in those times it was the way to express piety and faith in God; for those people, it was an opportunity to come close (*le-hitqarev*) to God.[23] Sacrifice may come across to us as being

20. Gunton, *Actuality of Atonement*, 165.

21. Halbertal, *On Sacrifice*, 10 and 117, n. 3. Thus, *li-qrov*, "to approach"; *le-hiqqarev*, "to bring close"; *le-haqriv*, "to carry forward"; *le-hitqarev*, "to come near"; *qerev*, "interior," "entrails," "inner"; *be-qerev*, "in the middle of," "inner," "among"; *be-qarov*, "soon," "impending"; and, *qarov*, "close," "relative."

22. The temple metaphor plays a considerable eschatological role, primarily in Orthodox Jewish prayer, and the Eucharist plays a crucial role in some Christian traditions. Yet neither Jews nor Christians use the actual sacrifice of real animals as a way to approach God.

23. Cf. the Greek word *prosphoron* (approximately, "that which is brought forward"), used in the Eastern Orthodox tradition to refer to the Eucharist.

a more or less alien behavior, but it need not necessarily be restricted to the past, or be something false, dangerous, or shocking.

(b) Regarding sacrificial terminology and thinking, there is reason to presume *a considerable discrepancy between what the church says—or is expected to say—and what many, many Christians in fact think and believe.* In the words of S. Mark Heim:

> Christians frequently conjure up an idea of sacrifice that we can half-believe long enough to attribute meaning to Christ's death. Once it has served that transitory purpose, we drop it as swiftly as possible, since we have no wider use for the category and do not know how to make sense of it.[24]

People who give pause before established ways of speaking about the crucifixion are told that their questions express doubt about the core and purpose of the Christian faith, its cornerstone, or at least one of its pillars. Three articles published in the *Tikkun* journal in the autumn of 2012 exemplify this attitude. Lawrence Swaim argued in the introductory article, "The Death of Christianity," that the cross was so problematic that it should not remain a Christian symbol. C. Kavin Rowe violently protested that view in his reply, "The Hope of the Cross." Anyone who retreated in such a manner from the cross, he argued, rejected Jesus and thereby all of Christianity. In the third article, "The Cross as a Central Christian Symbol of Injustice," Elisabeth Schüssler Fiorenza countered that the cross was a symbol of the injustices, abuses, and brutality—*the imperial injustice*—of the Roman empire.[25] These three articles jointly exemplify a commonly recurring phenomenon: strong reactions to critical questions and the fact that there are multiple interpretations and applications of the crucifixion of Jesus.

(c) Yet another aspect to consider in this context is the *relationship between religion and suffering.* Not all of the offerings described in the Hebrew Bible were animal sacrifices, yet it is the latter that are most familiar to the majority of readers of the Bible. There are many sections in the Hebrew Bible about animal sacrifice; in the New Testament there are both the narrative accounts in the Gospels and the Epistles, in which Jesus' suffering on

24. Heim, "Saved," 212.

25. See *Tikkun* (Autumn 2012): Swaim, "The Death of Christianity" (20–27), Rowe, "The Hope of the Cross" (28–29), and Schüssler Fiorenza, "The Cross as a Central Christian Symbol of Injustice" (30–32). See also the four attitudes described by Heim in *Saved from Sacrifice*, x.

the cross is described as a sacrifice.[26] The question that bothers many people is then: If Jesus' suffering and death are described in positive wording in the Christian tradition, why do we not now accept suffering and death as something good and useful? Is suffering something we should still strive for? What is the consequence of this chain of thought with regard to, for example, current attitudes toward torture?[27] If Jesus came in order to leave, if he were born to die, if he lived to suffer—why then should suffering today be something to be avoided or dismissed? *Redemptive violence,* or the issue of whether violence can ever be liberating or rehabilitating, is the subject of an ongoing intense discussion.[28] The *passion* is the name given to Jesus' final days, as described and defined by his pain (Latin *passio*, "suffering"). Elizabeth A. Castelli and other scholars have observed that there is a relationship between, on the one hand, the understanding that Jesus gave his life and, on the other hand, the view of martyrdom held by the first generations of Christians. She noted that those who see themselves as martyrs may not see the suffering of others. From this follows that those who are willing to sacrifice themselves may also be prepared to sacrifice others.[29]

Of course, we must immediately stress the great differences between the animal sacrifices in the sacrificial cults of antiquity and the death of Jesus, seen as a sacrifice. The ritual of animal sacrifice was meant to be carried out as quickly and painlessly as possible.[30] Theological emphasis was not

26. An example of a text on animal sacrifice in the Hebrew Bible is Lev 1–7. The body and deeds of Jesus are described as a sacrifice in, for example, John 17:19; and Gal 1:4; 2:20; Eph 5:2; Heb 7:27; 9:14; 10:14; and 1 John 2:2.

27. The relationship between torture (especially during the period 1973 to 1990, when General Augusto Pinochet was in power in Chile) and Christian communion has been researched by Cavanaugh; see *Torture and Eucharist*.

28. E.g., Brock, "The Cross of Resurrection and Communal Redemption." Following Mel Gibson's film, *Passion of the Christ,* this discussion intensified further, e.g., Corley and Webb, eds., *Jesus and Gibson's*; Cunningham, ed., *Pondering the Passion*; Plate, ed., *Re-Viewing the Passion*; Noel and Johnson, eds., *Passion of the Lord;* and Fredriksen, ed., *On the Passion*. This last book is, for the most part, identical with *Perspectives on the Passion*.

29. Castelli, *Martyrdom*, 196 and 201. See also Svartvik, "Gör detta," *Minne och manipulation*, 35–51 and Moss, *Myth of Persecution*, especially 247–60. See, too, the summary in the final chapter of this book of Rowan Williams's critical views of a theology that isolates Good Friday from Easter.

30. A distinction can be made between "rite" and "ritual." In this book, a rite is an act that is carried out according to a ritual; a ritual is thus a kind of instruction for the carrying out of a rite. Cf. Snoek, "Defining 'Rituals,'" *Theorizing Rituals*, 13–14: "A *rite* is the performance of an indivisible unit of ritual behavior. . . . A *ritual* is a prescription

put on the animal's *suffering*, yet the suffering of Jesus has in itself become the core of extensive aspects of the history of Christian thought.[31] In short, a crucifixion was slow and painful—precisely what was to be avoided in a sacrificial rite. As observed by Daniel C. Ullucci,

> I argue that the interpretation of animal sacrifice as an egregiously violent act is a modern myth, largely propagated by Christian interpreters seeking to more closely equate Jesus' violent death with animal sacrifice. Classical evidence . . . shows concern for minimization of violence, ritual control, and a lack of focus on the actual death of the animal.[32]

This insight makes it even more important to investigate the relationship between the view of suffering in Christian tradition and the passion for the Christian message.

(d) It is a well-known fact that there has often been an *anti-Jewish leaning* in Christian theology.[33] It has been expressed in a number of ways. The proceeding against Jesus as described in New Testament Gospels is unfortunately often presented in a manner that turns it into an accusation against the Jewish people. Holy Week has been anything but holy for Jews in Christian parts of the world.[34] Pogroms during Passion Week cannot be divorced from Christian presentations of the passion.[35]

Sometimes Judaism is defined as Old Testament (as if Judaism had lost its spiritual power and ability to develop by the time of the life and death of Jesus), and sometimes the Hebrew Bible's content is described as an ill-intentioned contradiction of the New Testament's message.[36] This

---

(written or otherwise) for a particular ceremony."

31. For an analysis of suffering as criterium, see Demetrius Williams, "Identifying," 92. "Paul's cross terminology is never directly related to suffering. . . . There is no hint of masochistic delight in suffering and death."

32. Ullucci, *Christian Rejection*, 154 n.16.

33. E.g., Carroll, *Constantine's Sword* and Nirenberg, *Anti-Judaism*, specifically 48–134. For investigations into the way Jews have been portrayed in Christian art, see Claman, *Jewish Images* and Kessler and Nirenberg, eds., *Judaism and Christian Art*.

34. Holy Week and Passion Week are names for the week between Palm Sunday and Easter.

35. One of the most bizarre practices of Christian anti-Jewish history must be the liturgical slapping of a Jew on Good Friday as punishment for the death of Jesus, e.g., Flannery, *Anguish*, 86–87.

36. In the words of John T. Pawlikowski, these views see the Hebrew Bible as either "a foretaste of Christian belief" or "the opposite of Christian faith." See *Christian-Jewish Relations*, 18.

anti-Jewish discourse also finds expression in discussions of sacrifice. The sacrificial cult in the Hebrew Bible is described as a *preliminary stage* (right and proper only during a specific period), *fragmentary* (never achieving true reconciliation), or even *erroneous* (incompatible with the Christian view of God). The words "I desire mercy, not sacrifice" appear twice in the Gospel of Matthew. Although this is undeniably a quote from the book of the prophet Hosea in the Hebrew Bible, it is often presented by Christian readers in contradiction, pitting Hebrew Bible against New Testament, and perhaps even Judaism's sacrificial worship of the time against the message of mercy of Christianity.[37] In this book we will see that such false contradictions cannot be supported.

If one looks up the Swedish word for sacrifice, or *offer,* in the dictionary accompanying the Swedish translation Bible 2000, the definition of reconciliatory sacrifice explains that its "continual repetition demonstrates its imperfection," and that when "Jesus once and for all sacrificed himself, he put an end to the sacrificial services of the old covenant. . . . In the new covenant there are only spiritual offerings, . . . which consist of conveying oneself and one's song of praise as an offering to God." This language is extensively retrieved from the Epistle to the Hebrews, the New Testament book that compares Jesus to a number of figures and elements in the Jewish temple cult: he is likened to the high priest, to the sacrifice, and even to the veil in the temple, the piece of fabric that separated the inner room of the temple, the most holy place, from the outside, larger room of the temple, the holy place.[38]

It has already been observed that animal sacrifice is not how we, in our time, approach the divine. The literature on sacrifice is therefore often brief and confrontational. Interestingly, it is nonetheless possible to interpret these stereotypical and apologetic accounts by means of sacrificial terminology. It has been considered necessary to sacrifice Jewish texts (namely, the collection of texts Christians call the Old Testament), Judaism, and Jewry so that the New Testament, Christianity, and Christendom might have a future and hope. Many times, it seems, an unexpressed driving force has resulted in a *renouncing* of Judaism ("Judaism is devoid of spirituality") and

37. Hos 6:6. Cf. Matt 9:13 and 12:7. Note that Hos 6:6 is also cited in rabbinical literature, which could scarcely be characterized as distancing itself from Hebrew Bible, e.g., *Avot de-Rabbi Natan* 4.5. For further discussion, see Halbertal, *On Sacrifice*, 38.

38. For an investigation into the temple metaphor of the Epistle to the Hebrews and its implications for Jewish-Christian relations, see Svartvik, *Bibeltolkningen*, 42–49, and the further discussion in "Epistle to the Hebrews," 77–91.

the belief that Judaism must necessarily be *transformed* ("all Jews should become Christians"). The death of Jesus is often described as payment for the Old Testament sacrificial cult. The text about sacrifice in the dictionary of the Swedish Bible 2000 is an example. Christian faith and Christianity would thus be incompatible with Judaism and Jewry *post Christum*.

Christian theology can and should find sustenance and direction in the Jewish faith and tradition, not least in its interpretations of scripture. Jews and Christians are theologically and existentially united in that they read the same texts and in them find the fundamental message that comforts, teaches, encourages, and warns. Jewish-Christian relations, historically and in current inter-religious dialogue, are highly relevant to exegetical and theological accounts. The basic approach of this book is greatly influenced by Paul M. van Buren's series, *A Theology of the Jewish-Christian Reality*.

> No agreements on other matters could hold us together in the Way if we could not agree on one point about the One of whom we speak when we use the word *God*. The person of whom we speak is the One designated in the Scriptures as the Holy One of Israel and the God of Abraham, Isaac and Jacob. . . . We mean the God whom faithful Jews, including Jesus and his followers, have always prayed to and called upon. Regardless of how the word *God* is used or meant elsewhere and by others, for those on the Way it has always meant what it meant for Jesus, the LORD, the God of Israel.[39]

Christian theology should be written *in the presence of* the Other—*panim el-panim* (Hebrew for "face to face")—explicitly to take seriously the religious experience of others.[40] This applies especially to how we treat the issue of sacrifice, something that is common to all humankind; it also reminds us how close the Christian faith is to Jewish tradition. The words of Leo Baeck, written a hundred years ago, still apply: *Man muss die Juden kennen, wenn man das Evangelium verstehen will* (One must know Jews if one wants to understand the gospel).[41] Official statements and solemn declarations are insufficient. *The only way to come to terms with anti-Jewish theology is to get to know the Jewish faith and tradition.* It is very relevant to reconciliation and transformation.

39. Van Buren, *Theology*, 1.32.

40. Cf. Exod 33:11. "Thus the LORD used to speak to Moses face to face, as one speaks to a friend."

41. Baeck, "Harnacks Vorlesungen," *Monatsschrift*, 28. For additional viewpoints, see Svartvik, "Judisk tro," *Hela jorden är Herrens*, 65–67.

Reconciliation Theology and Religious Pluralism

What effect might a discussion of sacrificial and reconciliation theology have when viewing other religious traditions? The reconciliation motif is often presented as the main argument against developing a Christian theology of religions, or a Christian view of other religious traditions. We can imagine a number of models: Do I see the religious Other as an *enemy* who must be combated at all costs, as an *acquaintance* I politely greet when we meet a few times a year, as a *friend* I trustingly and expectantly seek out in tough times, or as an unfamiliar *relative* I am closer to than I really understand? Each of these express theological approaches to other religious traditions.[42] Those who see other devout people as theological opponents often argue for exclusivity, that only in Christianity are human beings forgiven their sins—rendering theology of religions instantly uninteresting or even inappropriate. Some even believe an inter-religious dialogue to be the opposite of the Christian gospel, which should be about knowing the "one Christ," the one on the cross. "For I decided to know nothing among you except Jesus Christ, and him crucified."[43]

Avoiding the theology-of-religions issue is not that easy, however. Even if we restrict ourselves to Jewish-Christian relations, important questions remain. Does the Hebrew Bible express a vital, genuine relationship between the God of Israel and God's Israel? If so, when did this ancient covenant become outdated? Was there a best-before date, and if so, when was it? Was it when Jesus was born, or when he was performing miracles and teaching? Did it occur at the time of his Last Supper, or of his death? Was it when Christians began to believe Jesus had risen or at the fall of the temple in year 70? Why should it be important to *read* and respect the Hebrew Bible, but completely irrelevant to *listen* to the people who even today regularly gather to read it, in Hebrew? A Christian theology of religions must therefore begin by meeting the Jewish religious tradition. Jewish-Christian relations are not the *most important* issue for all Christians, but it is necessarily the *first* one.

There are certainly more aspects to consider in this context, but these items will have to suffice to illustrate the complexity of the matter. Do we know enough about the sacrifices that are described in the Bible, particularly the animal sacrifices? In what other ways might we view sacrifice?

42. For additional viewpoints, see Svartvik, "'Jag är Josef.'"

43. 1 Cor 2:2.

What is the relationship between religion and suffering? How might we be understood or explain how Christian reconciliation theology has been unable to reconcile with Judaism and Jews?

How do we proceed? Guiding this book is the observation that serious divisions have inadvertently occurred. (a) *The theology of the cross should not be isolated from other parts of Christian theology.* The history of the passion, of the suffering of Jesus, must not be separated from the story of Jesus' life, that is, his suffering must not be known in isolation from his teaching, and his life and death must not be separated from Christian belief in the resurrection.[44] (b) *Nothing is served by simply severing the Hebrew Bible from the New Testament,* for example by arguing that an alleged Old Testament religion of laws would be the total opposite of a New Testament faith, characterized by grace. Putting the historical context of Jesus—the historical experience and theological insights of his own people—in contrast with his theology is irresponsible. (c) *The content of the message must not be divorced from its effect.* What consequences are there then for Christian preaching about the crucifixion and Christian reconciliation? Does it lead to transformation?

Reconciliation and Transformation

Our main focus in this book will be to study some of the biblical passages about the death of Jesus on the cross with specific emphasis on reconciliation and transformation. But first, in chapter 3, we will look at the sacrificial theology of the Hebrew Bible and the types of sacrifice that are described in the first seven chapters of Leviticus. Only then can we, in the fourth chapter, study early Christian understanding of the temple's sacrificial cult. At the writing of the earliest texts of the New Testament, the temple in Jerusalem still existed. Did beliefs about the temple change after it was destroyed in year 70? What can we conclude about the views of Jesus and Paul on the temple? A number of critical questions are posed in the fifth chapter. What consequences do our beliefs about capital punishment have for our interpretations of the death of Jesus? Or, the opposite: how does Christian belief in the death of Jesus affect our understanding of capital punishment? Another question addresses the fact that Jesus died such a violent death. Christians believe that, in addition to Jesus' life and teaching, his death is one of the most prominent pillars of the Christian religion. What are

44. Belousek, *Atonement*, 18.

the consequences of associating God's ties to humanity with such a brutal event? What do Christians mean when they say the true nature of God is revealed on Golgotha? In the sixth and seventh chapters, two motifs are investigated that have come to play a crucial role in the Christian discussion of reconciliation: the broken-down dividing wall referred to in the second chapter of Ephesians and the torn veil of the temple described in three of the Gospels. How have these texts been interpreted traditionally, and are there other possible interpretations? In the eighth chapter, the consequences are presented and discussed. Where does this long and arduous path, through sacrifice in the Hebrew Bible and the life, suffering, death, and resurrection of Jesus in the New Testament, lead? What consequence can these texts have for you? The final chapter has been titled "Transformation" because it is about the importance of the belief in the resurrection in Christian tradition and for Christian self-conception. That Christians the world over worship on Sundays is a result of the Christian belief in the resurrection. Easter Sunday—Easter Vigil—is the Christian *festum festorum* (Latin for feast of feasts). What are the consequences for *reconciliation* and *transformation* that the events of Good Friday are understood in light of the message of Easter Sunday? First, let us study reconciliation and transformation, starting with the Hebrew Bible and Jewish theology.

3

Reconciliation as the Central Motif

As PREVIOUSLY STATED, IT is not through sacrifice—and especially not through animal sacrifice—that today's reader of the Bible comes to God. In other words, there is an eminent risk that the reader has an anachronistic approach to understanding sacrifice. It is imperative, therefore, that we present the fundamental concepts of biblical sacrificial theology. In his book *On Sacrifice,* Moshe Halbertal argues that there is a fundamental distinction between sacrificing as a gift to the divine, *to give sacrifice to someone,* and abstaining from something for a higher purpose, *to sacrifice oneself for something or someone.*[1] Halbertal observes that the latter meaning exists neither in the Bible nor in rabbinical Hebrew. The Hebrew word *qorban* (offering) today has a third meaning in addition to the previous two: *qorban* in modern Hebrew also means "victim."[2]

Halbertal's primary goal is to clarify the first two meanings: *sacrifice as a gift* and *sacrifice as self-sacrifice.* There is always the risk of a dichotomy becoming overly categorical, of course, but this division is elucidating.[3] In the first half of the book, he develops the reasoning that a person who sacrifices *to* someone reinforces an existing relationship. That which we call

1. In making his argument, Halbertal comments in passing on Mauss's *Gift*, but rejects that author's thesis—that gifts are not devoid of expectations of a *quid pro quo*—by reasoning that is it not applicable to the relationship between God and humanity; see Halbertal, *On Sacrifice*, 11: "In the human-divine relationship, the divine privilege to reject is rooted in the fact that the sacrifice is actually an act of returning rather than giving. God is entitled, as the one who gave the produce in the first place, to refuse its return."

2. Halbertal, *On Sacrifice*, 1–5 and 33. Cf. the following expression in Yiddish, in which the Hebrew word *qorban* is assigned a similar meaning: *a mentsh mit an eidelen gevisn qen nor zain a qorbn* (a person with a pure conscience can only be a victim), e.g., *Judiska ordspråk*, 78.

3. Ullucci criticizes attempts to find "some essential deep meaning that is universal to all sacrificial practice," see "Contesting," 60–61 and 70–71 n.13.

sacrifice is here the confirmation of a solidarity or love that far exceeds an exchange of services between two parties. This kind of sacrifice is thus *an expression of a previously existing relationship.*

In the second half of the book, Halbertal describes the phenomenon of sacrificing oneself *for* something, that is, to act unselfishly. The purpose is often to overcome the ego, to sacrifice oneself. In that context, he discusses martyrdom and war, which are two important and interconnected expressions of sacrifice as self-sacrifice for a noble cause.[4] Halbertal offers the example of the concept of sacrifice in war—self-sacrifice for something—by referring to the *Gettysburg Address*, Abraham Lincoln's famous speech at the dedication of a cemetery given on November 19, 1863, in which Lincoln stated, "These dead shall not have died in vain."[5] The reasoning is that the fallen soldiers had *sacrificed themselves* for an important purpose, that they had *been sacrificed* by their superiors for a greater purpose. This reasoning is even clearer in another of Lincoln's texts, one that Halbertal does not discuss in his book. Though less well known, it is nonetheless poignant. The president wrote a letter in 1864 to a mother who had lost several sons on the battlefield.[6]

> Executive Mansion,
> Washington, Nov. 21, 1864
>
> Dear Madam,
>
> I have been shown in the files of the War Department a statement of the Adjutant General of Massachusetts that you are the mother of five sons who have died gloriously on the field of battle. I feel how weak and fruitless must be any word of mine which should attempt to beguile you from the grief of a loss so overwhelming. But I cannot refrain from tendering you the consolation that may be found in the thanks of the Republic they died to save. I pray that

4. Halbertal, *On Sacrifice*, 114.

5. Abraham Lincoln, quoted in Halbertal, *On Sacrifice*, 102.

6. Lincoln's letter to Mrs. Bixby was printed in the *Boston Evening Transcript* on November 25, 1864, the same day as it was given to her personally by William Schouler. For additional viewpoints and a study of Lincoln's manner of relating and referring to biblical texts, see Freed, *Lincoln's Political Ambitions*, 60. See also testimonial by Lincoln's seamstress, Elizabeth Keckley, *Behind the Scenes*, 50. It later turned out that the information Lincoln had received was incorrect. Only two of her sons had been killed. Charles N. Bixby on May 3, 1863, and Oliver C. Bixby on July 30, 1864; see Basler, *Collected Works*, 8, 116–17. See also Bullard, *Abraham Lincoln*.

our Heavenly Father may assuage the anguish of your bereavement and leave you only the cherished memory of the loved and lost, and the solemn pride that must be yours *to have laid so costly a sacrifice upon the altar of Freedom.*

Yours, very sincerely and respectfully,

A. Lincoln

The closing line of the letter (italicized here) expresses this thought clearly: the death of the sons was a *sacrifice* that their mother *sacrificed* for freedom and her country in order to save the nation from division. It is a clear example of Halbertal's second category of sacrifice: *sacrifice as self-sacrifice.*

Sacrifice and Uncertainty

One of the most influential thinkers in the discussion of what sacrifice is and conveys is René Girard. He and his disciples have written extensively about violence and anger as important, even necessary, elements of the ritual of sacrifice.[7] Sacrifice in the meaning of self-sacrifice for a higher purpose certainly has much to do with violence. In a war situation, citizens are called to sacrifice themselves for their country. Halbertal argues, however, that the feelings that are in focus when we speak of *sacrifice as a gift* are not anger but rather uncertainty, insecurity, and anxiety. Is my sacrifice pleasing? Will it be received? According to Halbertal, this fundamental uncertainty characterizes the sacrifice: It is not payment for a good or a service; instead, it is a *gift*. Those who pay for themselves are not indebted and have rights, but those who present a gift are always uncertain as to how well it will be received.

The feeling of being disdained can turn to anger and resentment. The best known example in the Bible can be found in the fourth chapter of Genesis. "And the Lord had regard for Abel and his offering, but for Cain and his offering he had no regard. So Cain was very angry, and his countenance fell."[8] The account ends with Cain slaying his brother Abel. Here we have an

7. Girard, *Violence*, e.g., 1–2 and 25. For an overview of his contribution to biblical exegesis, see Goodhart and Astell, "Substitutive Reading."

8. Gen 4:4–5. See Halbertal, *On Sacrifice*, 115. For different interpretations of the story of Cain and Abel, see Svartvik, *Skriftens ansikten*, 12–30.

example of anger and violence—but instead of the actual sacrifice being the cause, it is the feeling of being scorned.

It would be worthwhile to further consider this because the opinion is often expressed in the general debate that violence, by definition, is the fundamental concept of a sacrificial cult, and that Christian belief fortunately means an end to this violent cult of sacrifice. Girard's influence here is striking: he argues that sacrifice forms the essence of all religions, and that all sacrifice is violent by definition, because it unconditionally demands the ritual death of an innocent victim. According to Girard, only Christianity has managed to break free from this sacrificial way of thinking. He contrasts what he calls "the ritualism of the Pharisees" with the teachings of Jesus, which he says promote mercy instead of sacrifice. Unfortunately, this is neither the first nor the last time the words of the Jewish prophet Hosea were used *against* Jewish piety: "For I desire steadfast love and not sacrifice."[9]

This manner of argumentation is difficult to understand and even more difficult to defend. As we will see in this chapter, not all the sacrifices that are described in the Bible were animal sacrifices, which is why it cannot be claimed that violence is what is common to sacrificial rituals, at least not in the Bible. Girard's overarching thesis asserts more than it explains. The sacrifices made by humans to God in the Bible can be characterized as different ways of *recompensing* God for what they had received. "For all things come from you, and of your own have we given you."[10] There is much evidence, in other words, that Halbertal is correct: The phenomenon of sacrifice-as-gift has primarily to do with uncertainty.

This also means we distort the concept of sacrifice if we describe it as a business transaction in which one party pays for the other party's good or service. When giving a gift, there is always the risk, and therefore a fear, that the gift will be rejected. That is what makes a gift a gift. One way of limiting the risk is to develop and follow a ritual. Halbertal writes:

> *Ritual is thus a protocol that protects from the risk of rejection. . . .* Ritual is an attempt to grapple with the inherent unpredictability of rejection.[11]

9. Hos 6:6.

10. 1 Chr 29:14. The Latin expression *do ut des* (I give that you may give) sometimes arises in the discussion of sacrifice. As we have seen that there is reason to claim that the fundamental concept in the Bible is that sacrifice is a *gift*, the Latin expression is not particularly apt—that is, as long as we do not see it as a dictum from God's perspective: God gives that people shall return the gift.

11. Halbertal, *On Sacrifice*, 15 and 18. See also 22.

In short, the answer to the uncertainty that is unavoidably related to sacrifice-as-gift is the ritual, which regulates how human beings are to carry out the sacrifice. Halbertal rejects the premise that sacrifice and violence are unconditionally interconnected. Instead, he claims that ritual and violence are two different reactions to the fundamental fear of being rejected.[12] Accordingly, ritual is a means of avoiding the violent reaction that might result if the feeling of being rejected were to arise. Religious rites help the religious person handle feelings of being alone and abandoned. In sum, *sacrifice is not an expression of, but rather an alternative to, violence.*

More Than Sin Offerings in the Bible

It is crucial to study the different types of offerings that are described in the first seven chapters of Leviticus. Regrettably, it appears to be the custom in many settings to speak disparagingly of the sacrificial theologies of the Hebrew Bible.[13] The two main reasons for this, and we have already touched upon them, are most likely a feeling of *alienation* from sacrificial rites in general combined with the belief that they are *obsolete,* since many people take it for granted that Jesus, through his death, has replaced the sacrificial cult of the Hebrew Bible. To speak knowledgeably and familiarly of the old ways could be seen as a questioning of the new. Finding fault and error in the old seems for some people to be a way to honor the new. Many presentations close with a sweeping and apologetic statement that Jesus fulfills or ends the Old Testament cult.

Yet there may be no surer or faster way to misunderstand the Good Friday theologies of the New Testament than to belittle the sacrificial regulations of the Hebrew Bible. That is why it is so important to become familiar with

12. Halbertal, *On Sacrifice*, 3. These questions naturally raise other questions Christians have about what is required for a Christian worship service to truly be the *Lord's* Holy Communion: What kind of bread must be used? How shall we define "the fruit of the vine"? Must the officiant be a man? The intensity of the discussion is not because communion has to do with the violent death of Jesus; rather, there is reason to believe that the strong feelings instead come from a desire to do things correctly, to strive to perform the ritual the right way, because performing a ritual improperly gives rise to misgivings. On the question of the ordination of women, see Svartvik, *Textens tilltal*, 49–70 and Ruether, *Introducing Redemption*, 81: "If women cannot represent Christ, in what sense can it be said that Christ represents women? Does this not mean that Christ does not redeem women, but re-enforces women's bondage in a patriarchal social system?"

13. This is pointed out in Gary Anderson, "Sacrifice," 1150.

the words on sacrifice in Leviticus. The following introduction to the most common sacrifices will, however, be very brief.[14]

The category that is first mentioned in Leviticus is *burnt offering*.[15] The Hebrew for this kind of sacrifice is *'olah*, which is related to the verb, "to rise," "to get up" (Hebrew *la-'alot*) because it literally "went up" in smoke as it was thoroughly and completely burned.[16] Burnt offerings were made in the morning and evening at the temple of Jerusalem. The Greek term for this kind of sacrifice is *holokauston (holos*, "thoroughly and completely," *kaustos* from *kaiein*, "to burn"). It is worth mentioning here that the Hebrew word *Shoah* (finite form: *ha-Shoah*, which means "destruction," "calamity") is preferable to the word Holocaust used for the Nazi genocide of six million Jews. This is because the Greek word *holokauston* is the term for a rite that God has ordained, "an offering by fire of pleasing odor to the LORD."[17]

The second category of sacrifice that is named is a *grain offering*, which is called *minchah*.[18] This was a sacrifice made of flour and oil that was salted. "You shall not omit from your grain offerings the salt of the covenant with your God; with all your offerings you shall offer salt."[19] That is why salt often plays an important role at Jewish meals, especially at Friday Sabbath. Today, *minchah* is the term used for the daily Jewish afternoon prayer.[20]

The third category is an *offering of well-being*, which in Hebrew is called *zevach shelamim*, often shortened to *shelamim*.[21] It is sometimes

14. Contrary to many other presentations of reconciliation in the Bible, this study does not investigate the sacrificial ritual of Yom Kippur, the Day of Atonement in Lev 16. The fundamental principles that are revealed in the study of Lev 1–7 are also applicable to the sacrificial ritual of Yom Kippur, the Day of Atonement. For one thing, animal sacrifice was not the only way to communicate forgiveness and reconciliation; for another, there were sacrifices for purposes other than just reconciliation. For a review of sacrificial ritual of the Day of Atonement in current and biblical writings, see Larsson, *Tid för Gud*, 82–106.

15. Lev 1.

16. Milgrom, *Leviticus 1–16*, 133–77 and Milgrom, *Leviticus*, 21–24.

17. "Holocaust" became the established name when the television series of the same name aired.

18. Lev 2. Milgrom, *Leviticus 1–16*, 177–202 and Milgrom, *Leviticus*, 25–27.

19. Lev 2:13.

20. On Fridays, these prayers are read immediately before the *qabbalat shabbat* (receiving the sabbath), then followed by the evening prayer: *ma'ariv* (cf. *'erev*, "evening"). (Besides the afternoon and evening prayers, there is a morning prayer called *shacharit*.)

21. Lev 3 and 7:11–34. Milgrom, *Leviticus 1–16*, 202–25 and Milgrom, *Leviticus*, 28–29. For suggested translations, see e.g., Baruch A. Levine, *Leviticus*, 15, and Modéus, *Sacrifice*, 358.

called "peace offering" (cf. *shalom*, "peace"). This sacrifice was in part burned, in part consumed by the priests, and in part fed to the person making the sacrifice and to that person's family. In other words, it was a sacrifice that contributed greatly to human community. It was to be immediately consumed: "And the flesh of your thanksgiving sacrifice of well-being shall be eaten on the day it is offered; you shall not leave any of it until morning."[22] This sacrifice had nothing to do with sin. The next category of sacrifice did, however.

This kind of sacrifice is the one most familiar to Christians, in English called a *sin offering*. Its Hebrew name is *chattat*.[23] This sacrifice was presented when a person had sinned *without intent*. The key term in Hebrew is *bish-gagah*, which can be translated as "unintentionally" or "unknowingly."[24] *For intentional sins there was no sacrifice*. This is an important indication that neither the sinner nor the sin per se was in focus here; rather, the ritual consequences of the sin were what mattered.[25] The cultic impurity was removed by the sin offering. In other words, neither God nor the person offering was the object of the verb "to reconcile." Rather, the *sanctum* was purified. In sum, God was not reconciled, but the sin was removed. Jacob Milgrom argues that this is why *chattat* should be translated as "purification offering" rather than "sin offering": it is an act of *cleansing*.[26] In sum, there were many more kinds of offerings than sin offerings (which shows that sacrifice was not just about sin), and there were sins for which no offering was acceptable (because there only existed offerings for unintentional sins).

The final type of sacrifice described in the introductory chapters of Leviticus is the *guilt offering*.[27] In Hebrew it is called *asham* and was offered by someone who, for example, took something unintentionally from the temple. It was to replace that which was taken and add a fifth of the value. This sacrifice was also offered by people who committed perjury. Milgrom has proposed it be called a "reparation offering."[28]

22. Lev 7:15.

23. Lev 4:1–5:13. See also Num 15:22–31. Milgrom, *Leviticus 1–16*, 226–318 and Milgrom, *Leviticus*, 30–45.

24. Lev 4:2. Cf. 4:13: "unintentionally and the matter escapes the notice of the assembly."

25. E.g., Lev 16:16 and 15:31.

26. Milgrom, *Leviticus*, 30.

27. Lev 5:14–6:7.

28. Milgrom, *Cult*, 18. The primary text in the Bible is Lev 5:14—6:7. For further viewpoints, see Milgrom, *Leviticus 1–16*, 319–78 and Milgrom, *Leviticus*, 46–61. A

In sum, the offerings were a way to manifest various aspects of the relationship between God and humans. Not every offering was a sin offering, nor is every Christian prayer always and solely about confessing sins. "Thanks," "help," and "forgiveness" are sometimes said to be the three main words in prayer. We could perhaps say the same of the sacrifices in the temple. The sacrifices are sometimes said to have had three main purposes: *expressing well-being, offering a gift,* and *indicating reconciliation.*[29] We have already said that the most fundamental aspect of sacrifice is "to come near." Sacrifice was the way people of that time approached the divine to say "thanks," "help," and "forgive."

In this chapter it has been clarified that animal sacrifice was not the only way to communicate forgiveness and reconciliation and that there were offerings for purposes other than just reconciliation. Sacrifice and reconciliation can be described as two circles that only partially overlap, because *sacrifice was not the only response to sin and guilt, and sin and guilt were not the only reason to sacrifice.* There were not only sin offerings (if for simplicity's sake, despite Milgrom's objections, we choose to translate *chattat* as "sin offering"). If these were not offerings for all sins, then the sin offering was not what we seem to think it was. The ritual was not imperative, but it meant that the person was forgiven and granted reconciliation by means of the sacrifice.[30] It is ultimately God's conduct that is described in the ritual: *God* is at work in the rite. Sacrifice was an expression of a renewed divine faith in humanity. The descriptions in the Bible are incomplete in describing the opportunities human beings have for *reconciliation* and *transformation.*[31]

---

review of the literature reveals that it is notoriously difficult to differentiate between *chattat* and *asham*. See, however, Milgrom, *Cult*. The offerings referred to in Mark 1:44, Matt 8:4, and Luke 5:14 should have been *asham*, because it was the type offered by a person who had been cleansed of the condition that has incorrectly been translated as leprosy. See Lev 14:10–31, and especially 12–14. Even sin offerings and burnt offerings were offered on this occasion; see vv. 19, 22, and 30–31.

29. This is how Halbertal characterizes Smith, *Lectures*, see *On Sacrifice*, 13–14.

30. E.g., *Mishnah Yoma* 8.9.

31. Cf. Jay Sklar, quoted in Belousek, *Atonement*, 196: "As in the New Testament, then, God shows his grace not only by granting forgiveness, but by providing sinners with the means of forgiveness to begin with."

Confirming the Relationship with God

In studying this sacrificial theology, we see that *first* there existed a relationship between two parties, *then* a sacrifice was made. The sacrifices were the expressions of a preexisting relationship. This relationship was not *constituted* by the sacrifice; it was *confirmed* by it. In other words, this was not about humans *entering* into a covenant; rather, it was about *remaining* in the covenant. The sacrificial offering was not a vehicle that allowed humans to *earn* a relationship with God; rather, it was primarily an expression of humans wanting to *devote* something to God.

When Jerusalem fell and the temple was destroyed, a radical change took place. We will study this next. How were Jewish and Christian *theologies* affected by this *historic* event?

4

Why Did the First Christians Stop Making Sacrifices?

WHY DID PEOPLE STOP sacrificing in the temple of Jerusalem? The purpose of this chapter is to respond to this seemingly simple question. Many people would immediately agree that *Jews* stopped sacrificing, quite simply because the temple was destroyed by the Romans on the 9th day in the Jewish month of *av* in year 70. But why did *the first Christians* stop making sacrifices? The answer to this question is normally *formulated theologically* rather than *explained historically*. Many people would probably say that Christians stopped sacrificing because after Jesus' death, sacrifices were no longer needed. Was his death not the ultimate sacrifice? Was not the destruction of the temple thirty years later the historical confirmation of a theological fact? It becomes apparent that the question is answered differently—historically or theologically—depending on whether we are discussing a sacrifice made by Jews or Christians. That is why in the current chapter we will ask the question: *Why did the first Christians stop making sacrifices?*

We have already seen that the death of Jesus is often likened to the sacrifices in the temple, but there are many possible approaches. There has never existed a single Christian theology of the cross. There have always been different ways of describing what happened and what the consequences were of Jesus' death. David F. Ford has listed a number of spheres from which descriptive images and terms are drawn: the sacrificial cult, the judicial system, war, the marketplace, family relations, medicine, history, politics, friendship, and nature are some of them.[1] One of these spheres is that of the sacrifices in the Jerusalem temple. We need to study how the first Christians felt about the sacrificial cult in Jerusalem. What do we know of the views in the early Christian movement of the temple and its worship services?

1. Ford, *Self*, 3. See also Guroian, *Melody*, 44.

Historical Circumstance or Theological Reason?

Theologically, it is more or less customary to claim that the life, teachings, and death of Jesus spelled the end of the sacrificial cult. To recall the definition of the word "sacrifice" in the glossary of the Swedish Bible 2000: "When Jesus once and for all sacrificed himself, he put an end to the sacrificial rituals of the old covenant."[2] Categorical statements of this sort require moderation, of course. Ullucci has observed that it took a surprisingly long time for Christians to formulate a theological response to the cessation of the sacrificial cult.[3] The reason, he suggests, for the delayed response was that Christians were forced to find new explanations for something that had been accepted as fact, namely, that the temple no longer existed. Had the Christian movement been genuinely and uniformly critical of the temple from the beginning, or even noticeably anti-temple, it would have been difficult to understand why it took so long for Christian authors to find and formulate good arguments for their position.[4] Ullucci has studied a large number of early Christian texts, among them Paul's epistles, the Gospels, the Epistle of Barnabas, and the writings of Justin Martyr, Clement of Alexandria, and Cyprian of Carthage. He concludes it was not for *theological* reasons that Christians first rejected sacrifice and then lived according to this conviction. Rather, there were *historical* circumstances that effectively forced Christianity to become a nonsacrificing religion. "In one sense," Ullucci writes, "early Christians stopped sacrificing for the completely mundane reason that there was no place to do so."[5] Christians were compelled to provide a *theological* explanation for the *historical* situation—which was that there no longer existed a temple in Jerusalem. This insight is reminiscent of James Parkes's observation that good theology cannot be built on bad history.[6] Our first step must be to study the early Christian attitudes

2. Glossary in Swedish in Bible 2000, *s.v. offer.* See also the reference section, *s.v. offer.* "Enligt urkristen tro har emellertid Jesus en gång för alla försonat människorna med Gud och därmed gjort alla offer överflödiga (According to ancient Christian beliefs, however, Jesus once and for all reconciled human beings with God, thereby making all sacrifices superfluous)."

3. See Ullucci, "Contesting," 57–74 and his monograph *Christian Rejection*, specifically 65–118.

4. Ullucci, *Christian Rejection*, 134.

5. Ullucci, *Christian Rejection*, 135.

6. Parkes, "Reappraisal," 301: "Good theology cannot be built on bad history."

toward the worship services in the temple. Only then we can reflect on the situation and challenges of today.

The only New Testament author we can say with certainty wrote his text before the year 70 is Paul the apostle. Nothing indicates that he categorically rejected the temple and its sacrificial services. Rather, the opposite is true: he uses terminology taken straight from the sacrificial cult to describe the importance of the life and death of Jesus.[7] The importance of his missionary work, he writes, is "because of the grace given me by God to be a minister of Christ Jesus to the gentiles in the priestly service of the gospel of God, so that the offering of the gentiles may be acceptable, sanctified by the Holy Spirit."[8] In dictating what characterized a Christian life, he appeals to his spiritual brothers and sisters to present their bodies "as a living sacrifice, holy and acceptable to God."[9] Paul wrote this while the temple still existed and the daily sacrifices were still being offered. These statements can hardly be interpreted as a devastating criticism of the temple and its worship services. In his epistles to the Christians in Corinth, for example, Paul chose to direct his criticism toward the sacrificial cults in the area because they were *non-Jewish,* in other words, that the sacrifices being made were not being offered to the God of Israel. For Paul, the problem was not that the sacrifice itself was a *mistake* but rather that the sacrifices of the non-Jewish community there were *misdirected* because they were not being offered to the God of Israel.[10]

Post-Traumatic Theology?

One could describe the New Testament Gospels as being double-exposed. On the one hand, they are about Jesus' public life before the year 70. On the other hand, however, they are written after 70 (perhaps with the exception of the Gospel according to Mark, which is usually dated at around 70). In Matthew, Mark, and Luke, Jesus and his disciples are described participating in the worship services at the temple of Jerusalem.[11] The account of

7. E.g., Rom 3:24–25 and 1 Cor 5:7.

8. Rom 15:15–16.

9. Rom 12:1.

10. E.g., 1 Cor 8. See also Ullucci, *Christian Rejection*, 12, 133 and 155–56 n.26.

11. Mark 1:40–44; 14:12–25; 11:15–18; Matt 5:18; Acts 2:26; 3:1; 5:42; and 24:17. These references to Acts demonstrate that Jewish Christ-believers continued to worship in the temple up to the very end of the book of Acts. This participation in the cult existed

the temple cleansing is included in all four New Testament Gospels. The Gospel that was written last compares the resurrection of Jesus on the third day with a rebuilt temple.

> The Jews then said to him, "What sign can you show us for doing this [i.e., cleansing the temple]?"
>
> Jesus answered them, "Destroy this temple, and in three days I will raise it up."
>
> The Jews then said, "This temple has been under construction for forty-six years, and will you raise it up in three days?"
>
> But he was speaking of the temple of his body. After he was raised from the dead, his disciples remembered that he had said this; and they believed the scripture and the word that Jesus had spoken.[12]

We should ask if there was a connection between the fall of the temple and Johannine Christology, or who Jesus was and what he meant to Christians as expressed in the Gospel according to John. Could the Johannine way of formulating high Christology at least in part be described as a reaction to the fall of the temple? René Kieffer writes that the resurrection gave the disciples "a key to understanding the meaning of the cleansing of the temple."[13] Was there something we might call *post-traumatic theology*—that is, that Christians found new forms and means of expressing their beliefs without the temple of Jerusalem, given its destruction?[14]

Both the Jewish and the Christian traditions found ways to survive the catastrophe of the temple being destroyed in year 70. The royal road through Judaism can be described with the words, *and the flesh became*

alongside their thinking of and describing Jesus' death as a sacrifice, so the two do not seem to have been understood as mutually exclusive.

12. John 2:18–22. For an interpretation in which the historical Jesus might have understood himself as the temple of Jerusalem, see Perrin, *Jesus the Temple*. If forty-six years had passed since the renovation of the temple began in 20 BCE, this conversation would have taken place in the year 26 CE, that is, barely forty-six years (!) before the fall of the temple.

13. Kieffer, *Johannesevangeliet 1–10*, 72.

14. Kieffer, *Johannesevangeliet 1–10*, 73. See however Ullucci, *Christian Rejection*, 90: "The Judean temple cult, and animal sacrifice in general, are no major concerns in the gospel of John." A similar case is the epistle to the Hebrews, which is written either not long before or at most a decade after the fall of the temple. The epistle describes Jesus as the ultimate sacrifice. See Hebrews 7:23–25; 9:8–10; and 10:1–12. The epistle to the Hebrews should not be isolated from its historical context, either. For additional views, see Svartvik, "Reading the Epistle to the Hebrews."

word. In other words, temple worship with its many sacrifices ("flesh") was replaced by prayer, worship services in synagogues, and not least, studying scripture ("word"). Judaism thereby *sublimated* the temple sacrifices according to Halbertal: When reading from the Bible about sacrifice, it is "as if" (Hebrew *ke-ilu*) the sacrificial service goes on.[15] In his book, *The Talmud and the Internet*, Jonathan Rosen proposed that the writings and interpretations of the Talmud could be likened to a virtual temple.[16]

Christian tradition developed differently. Its reaction was rather, *and the Word became flesh*. Jesus of Nazareth is the one who embodies—incarnates—God's voice in the Bible. Both Jewish and Christian traditions in other words found a continuation of the sacrificial cult, but they did so in different ways.

Responses to the Fall of the Temple

With time, however, there developed several approaches to addressing the issue of the temple and its sacrificial services.[17] We could say that representatives of the Christian tradition eventually insisted that all sacrifice be *substituted*—in contrast to the Jewish tradition, better described as being *sublimated*—by the absolute and final sacrifice. The Epistle of Barnabas, which is usually dated to the years 80–130 CE, makes an argument against there being any value in a sacrificial cult. The Epistle of Barnabas is so supersessionist that the words of the Hebrew Bible completely lose their literal meaning. God's instructions in the Hebrew Bible are so allegorical that to use them as if they were about real tabernacles, temples, and sacrificial worship services would be to misunderstand them. God would never have been pleased by sacrifice. According to the Epistle of Barnabas, the entire temple cult was an enormous mistake.[18]

15. Halbertal, *On Sacrifice*, 4 and 7. On the concept of *ke-ilu*, see Svartvik, *Skriftens ansikten*, 167–69. In Orthodox Jewish prayer, the temple metaphor plays a role so significant that sacrifice may be better described as *suspended* rather than *sublimated*. Yet we should ask, what do people truly mean when praying about the Third Temple? Is it comparable with the Church of Sweden prayer, "May soon come the day when you shall create new heavens and a new earth where justice will reside?" See *Den svenska kyrkohandboken. Del I*, 145.

16. See Rosen, *Talmud and the Internet*, 105. On 54 and 82 he discusses "the flesh became words" and "the word became flesh" (cf. John 1:14).

17. Ullucci, *Christian Rejection*, 96–118.

18. Epistle of Barnabas 1–3 and 16. For more opinions, see Svartvik,

In his *Dialogue with Trypho, a Jew,* Justin Martyr (100–165 CE) expresses a different opinion. He claims the cult in Jerusalem was temporary. It was justified, but only for a specific period of time. God had always intended the temple to have a temporary existence. Its only purpose was to prevent the people of Israel from reverting to the worship of idols, but after Jesus, sacrifice was no longer needed. In other words, Justin argues that Israel was correct in interpreting scripture literally, but for a limited time only, which Israel should also have understood.[19] In sum, the Epistle of Barnabas and *Dialogue with Trypho, a Jew* present two completely different responses to the question of why Christians do not sacrifice.

Unlike Justin, but like the Epistle of Barnabas, Clement of Alexandria (145–214) argues that the instructions for sacrifice should always have been interpreted allegorically. The instructions are actually about Christian lifestyle and worship. Clement writes that living a life free of temptation (Greek *pathē*) was the proper offering to please God. Christian prayer was also a proper offering.[20] The Hebrew Bible verses on sacrifice were really about something else, that is, spiritual self-discipline and piety.

Yet another example of how differently the early Christian authors interpreted the writings on sacrifice is Cyprian of Carthage (d. 258). His epistles, written during a time of persecution, were followed up by a discussion of the validity of baptism and communion if performed by a priest or bishop who did not meet the criteria. Most relevant here is his criticism of Christians in North Africa, who seemed to have celebrated Communion with water instead of wine. When Cyprian retorts that the chalice must contain wine, he joined three symbols: Jesus' death is like the sacrifices in the temple, and Holy Communion is like a sacrifice, because the wine is like blood. In other words, Christian Communion corresponds to the animal sacrifices in the temple.[21]

This review of some of the early Christian writings indicates that there were many responses to the question of why Christians refrained from sacrificing. According to Ullucci, we have good reason to believe that Christians did not stop sacrificing voluntarily. Quite simply, the Christian movement was forced to become a nonsacrificing religion for *historical* reasons. Accounts following year 70, and increasingly with time, attempted to explain

"Ersättningsteologins historiska bakgrund."

19. Justin Martyr, *Dialogue with Trypho,* 22.

20. Clement of Alexandria, *Stromateis* 5.11 (67.1) and 7.6 (30–34).

21. Cyprian of Carthage, Epistles 67 and 73.

and rationalize the fact. It is apparent from the fact that Christian criticism of the temple was not uniform. Yes, Christian authors argued that the temple cult was incorrect, but they argued it was incorrect for different reasons, and *those reasons were incompatible.* Some authors wrote that it had always been incorrect to sacrifice, because the instructions in the Bible should have been interpreted allegorically. Others argued that temple sacrifice was correct for a period of time, but that Jesus was the true sacrifice and therefore, after his death, it became wrong to sacrifice. As Ullucci observes:

> The key thing to notice about these positions is that they do not cohere well. Did God never want animal sacrifice? Or is Jesus an animal sacrifice? Or are prayers better than sacrifice anyway? . . . [I]t is not even a logical chain of positions. It is a collection of different arguments from different periods and different authors all useful against different opponents (Romans, Judeans, other Christians, etc.).[22]

These are all *theological* responses to the historical circumstance of the temple being destroyed, while previously there existed another attitude toward the sacrificial cult. We have good reason to conclude that adherents of the earliest Christian movement *supported* the worship services held at the temple. In all likelihood, they mourned the fall of the temple on *tish'ah be-av* (the 9th [day] of [the month of] *av*), a day that is still marked in the Jewish calendar and observed as a day of fasting.

This is important to note, because in the Christian tradition the temple of Jerusalem is often described in a disconcerting way: *Descriptions of the temple before 70 are tinged with contempt, yet the importance of the temple after 70 is overemphasized.* On the one hand, we find the temple is often depicted in disparaging terms as an institution seeped in hypocrisy and corruption. The temple of Jerusalem has served as a metaphor for the abuse of power.[23] But to criticize an *abuse* is not the same as criticizing the *actual or intended* use. On the other hand, the role of the temple after its fall in 70 has been overemphasized, because the apologetic tradition claimed Jews could no longer obtain atonement, given that sacrifice had ceased. This is why we need to learn the opinions in the Jewish tradition toward the fall of the temple. The most famous exposition is the collection of writings called *Avot de-Rabbi Natan*:

22. Ullucci, "Contesting," 69.

23. E.g., Nirenberg, *Anti-Judaism*, 328–29.

> Rabbi Jochanan ben Zaqqai was walking one day with his disciple, Rabbi Jehoshua', near Jerusalem after the destruction of the Temple. Rabbi Jehoshua' observed the destroyed Temple and said: "Alas! The place that reconciled the sins of the people of Israel is in ruins." Rabbi Jochanan ben Zaqqai comforted him and said: "Grieve not, my son. There is yet another path to reconciliation that will serve us though the Temple is destroyed. We can be reconciled through acts of good will (Hebrew *gemilut chasadim*). For it is written: '*I desire steadfast love and not sacrifice.*'"[24]

Jewish tradition makes clear that it is possible to live a Jewish life after the fall of the temple. Studying the writings on sacrifice are *like* sacrificial services in the temple, daily prayer rises to heaven *as does* the smoke of burnt offerings, and good deeds are *in the manner of* sacrifice, as in Paul's dictate to the Christians in Rome: present your bodies "as a living sacrifice, holy and acceptable to God, which is your spiritual worship."[25] We should remember that already before the fall of the temple there was an established institution that served as the religious center for the Jewish people after 70, namely the synagogue and its worship services. What do we know about the synagogues at the time of Jesus, and what can we assume to be his likely attitude toward those worship services?

"He went to the synagogue on the sabbath day, as was his custom."

The heading is quoted from Luke 4:16 to remind us of an often-overlooked fact. Jesus of Nazareth was a pious Jew who celebrated the Jewish holidays, read from the Jewish holy scriptures, and prayed the Jewish prayers. We often say that Jesus was a Jew, but to what extent does it influence our view of his teachings and life? How often do we hear, for example, that he celebrated the Sabbath with his disciples every Friday evening? Or is his Jewish context mentioned in theological literature, preaching, and teaching almost exclusively to mark a *difference*—at best by disassociation, at worst by condemnation? This is yet another clear example of how *Jesus' historical context is systematically presented to serve as his theological contrast.*[26] Instead of

24. *Avot de Rabbi Natan* 4.5. The closing citation (italicized here) is from Hos 6:6. See also *Talmud Bavli Berakhot* 6b.

25. Rom 12:1.

26. One example of this type of contrasting historical description is Borg, *Conflict*.

providing an educational resource for understanding Jesus and the early Christian movement, Jewish beliefs and tradition are often presented as a theological problem to solve, not as a life to live.

What Would Jesus Do?

It is imperative that we situate Jesus, the first disciples, and the early Christian movement *within* the Judaism of their day if we are to understand them better. In an article published on the Jewish Day of Atonement in 2012, Paula Fredriksen asked a question that is particularly relevant to this book. *What Would Jesus Do?* Did Jesus celebrate Yom Kippur, the Day of Atonement?[27] It would be truly remarkable if the answer to that question were no. In recent surveys, 70 percent of Israeli Jews responded that they always fasted on Yom Kippur, and an additional 11 percent responded that they sometimes did.[28] In antiquity, we can be sure that pious Jews throughout the entire Roman Empire celebrated this holiday. Would Jesus truly be the only Jewish religious leader who did *not* celebrate Yom Kippur? That Jesus really did celebrate Yom Kippur is beyond all reasonable doubt, as there is no mention anywhere in historic sources that he did not celebrate

---

Borg argues that Jesus was unique in emphasizing compassion, in contrast to the other religious leaders of the time, who instead chose to speak of holiness (e.g., ibid., 135). Borg fails to observe the difference between the *halakhah* and *aggadah* genres, and therefore compares writings of different types, misconstruing both *halakhah* and *aggadah*. On 147–49, 154 and 173 he argues that the difference between Jesus and his environment is that Jesus maintains that holiness, not impurity, is contagious. It would have been interesting in this context to hear an analysis of "Watch out, and beware of the yeast of the Pharisees and Sadducees" (Matt 16:6; cf. Mark 8:15 and Luke 12:1). Though Borg explicitly and repeatedly claims that Jesus' opposition was only toward the Jewish elite, he still manages to be inconsistent. See, for example, p. 146, where he writes that the opponent was really all of "first-century Judaism," which would be completely absurd. In another example of unacceptable contrasting, the majority of Jews of the time are described sweepingly as shallow and preoccupied with the material world (ibid., 250): "Apparently, Jesus perceived most of his contemporaries as centered in the finite."

27. Fredriksen, "Yom Kippur: WWJD?" WWJD is the acronym for "What Would Jesus Do?" Rabbinical literature about *yoma* (Aramaic for "the day," that is, the Day of Atonement) describes above all what the high priest did on that day in the temple of Jerusalem. See Levine, *Ancient Synagogue*, 548. The majority of Jews (that is, those who did not live in Jerusalem and were not there because they were on pilgrimage for the Feast of Tabernacles, or Sukkot) probably celebrated Yom Kippur where they lived, as Jews do today by fasting, praying, confessing, and reading scripture.

28. Elazar, "How Religious Are Israeli Jews?"

it. Nothing in the Gospels indicates that Jesus was criticized for not fasting on the Day of Atonement. The silence on this issue can in this case be interpreted as a clear indication that Jesus in fact celebrated Yom Kippur. How did he do it? He certainly would have fasted for the specified twenty-five hours. Did he recite the appropriate prayers? Why would he not have prayed, first together with his family and then with his disciples? At that time, Jews in Galilee and all over the world gathered regularly in synagogues. The growth in the number of synagogues before the fall of the temple indicates that decentralization was occurring before 70. Naturally, the destruction of the temple was a national and religious catastrophe, but substantial aspects of the temple's function had been assumed by the synagogues, where people read, translated, and studied scripture and recited prayers. In sum, the synagogue was "a small sanctuary" (Hebrew *miqdash me'at*) long before the fall of the temple.[29]

Together with other Jews all over the world at that time, Jesus prayed to *avinu malkenu* (our father, our king), to "the father of mercies and the God of all consolation."[30] Fredriksen's question about how Jesus celebrated Yom Kippur is a valuable reminder to speak of the Jewish Day of Atonement in a manner that respects Jesus' own community of prayer.[31]

29. Ezek 11:16. For a comprehensive presentation of synagogue expansion, see Lee I. Levine, *Ancient Synagogue*, e.g., 80: "Centralization of the Temple was paralleled by a decentralization in the local synagogues. Prior to 70, the Temple was recognized as *the* central institution in Jewish life; nevertheless, the emerging synagogue had become the pivotal institution in local Jewish affairs. This parallel development in the first century was indeed fortuitous. Though no one could have foreseen the outcome, the seeds of Jewish communal and religious continuity had already been sown well before the destruction of the Temple."

30. 2 Cor 1:3. Jews recite the prayer *avinu malkenu* (in Isa 63:16 and 33:22) from Rosh Ha-shanah to Yom Kippur (except on the Sabbath); e.g., Millgram, *Jewish Worship*, 234–35.

31. An interesting topic, unfortunately beyond the horizon of this book, is the question of whether Jesus prayed to God on Yom Kippur for forgiveness for committed sins. Has this question been asked in Christian theology? We see how two fundamental concepts in Christian incarnation theology meet: On the one hand "God of God, light of light, true God of true God" and on the other hand, "has become human." There exists an inherent Christological tension in *totus Deus sed non totum Dei* (completely and wholly God, but not all that is God). How much of the history is there room for in high Christology, and how much high Christology can there be in the history? A relevant parallel may be the testimony in Matt 24:36. "But about that day and hour no one knows, neither the angels of heaven, *nor the Son,* but only the Father" (italics added).

5

"For Violence Is Not an Attribute of God"

In the previous chapter, we learned that the first Christians did not comprehend the death of Jesus as a repudiation of temple worship services. The last sentence in Luke's Gospel summarizes this view: "and they were continually in the temple blessing God."[1] It was only after the fall of the temple in 70 CE that a systematic disassociation began, a fact that Ullicci interprets as the expression of a *theological* adaptation to a completely new *historical* situation.

This chapter is devoted to one specific question: How have Christians perceived Jesus' suffering? How do Christians react to the fact that he died such a violent death? Our intent is to critically analyze the argument that violence and death are necessary conditions for reconciliation to take place. There is good reason to describe this as a shift in focus of Christians' interpretation of the death of Jesus. Instead of likening the crucifixion to temple sacrifice, it is presented as an event that unconditionally must be violent and result in death.

Is Capital Punishment a Crime?

Darrin W. Snyder Belousek's book, *Atonement, Justice, and Peace,* is nearly 700 pages long and in places quite technical, making it difficult to summarize in this limited context. One way to describe the purpose of the book is to focus on the question of capital punishment.[2] In Sweden, the last execution took place in 1910. Capital punishment was abolished from

1. Luke 24:53.

2. Belousek, *Atonement*, e.g., 27–29. For a discussion of capital punishment, see Berkowitz, *Execution*; Bergman, "Fighting the Death Penalty"; Schieber, *Justice and Mercy*.

Swedish law in times of peace and war in 1921 and 1973, respectively, and was made illegal in 1976: "Dödsstraff får icke förekomma" (The death penalty is forbidden).[3] In other words, several decades have passed since this decision was made in Sweden. The reintroduction of capital punishment is not on the agenda of any of the established political parties in Sweden. In Swedish political debate, capital punishment is a non-issue.

The situation is radically different in other countries, such as the United States, where capital punishment is a topic of discussion. Belousek teaches at Ohio Northern University. Capital punishment is practiced in the state of Ohio, though not as extensively as in other states, such as Texas. In a country where religion plays a major role in public debates and where capital punishment is a debated topic, the Bible can be cited in the ongoing discussion about the death penalty. Conflict can arise, Belousek notes, between the traditional interpretation of the crucifixion of Jesus and the individual Christian's belief against the sentencing and enforcing of the death penalty. The people who argue that Jesus *had to* die often emphasize that the sins of humankind brought on the death of Jesus, and only following his death was the temple veil torn, an event usually interpreted as opening the way to God after being closed to all previous generations. (We will return in the seventh chapter to how the tearing of the veil has been interpreted and could be interpreted.) In sum, according to this understanding, it is a theological necessity that Jesus die. Otherwise, there will be no atonement for humans' sins, God will not be appeased, God will remain wrathful, and humanity will be doomed. And if we must accept the death of Jesus as a penalty that is theologically necessary, why and how should Christians object to the death penalty today? Is not the death penalty just as necessary today to erase sin and atone for crime?[4] We could take this a step further: could the passion of Christ even be proof that God approves of the death penalty? Otherwise, why would so many Christians claim that "Jesus had to die"? And if so, by *imitatio Dei* (to imitate God), should not Christians insist that capital punishment be reintroduced in countries such as Sweden? Is there a difference between saying that a person who has been sentenced for heinous crimes "must die" and that "Jesus must die"? Those words in the Bible, "in that case you may even be

3. Regeringsformen Ch. 2. 4 § (law 1976:871). For more information about the death penalty in Swedish legislation, see the book published posthumously by Seth, *Överheten och svärdet*, and Bergman, *Dödsstraffet*.

4. Cf. Rom 6:23: "For the wages of sin is death" (Greek *ta gar opsōnia tēs hamartias thanatos*).

found fighting against God!"—are they applicable here?[5] If God approves of capital punishment, who would then oppose it?

If, on the other hand, the question of capital punishment today elicits a resounding No! then how does that affect the view of the death of Jesus two thousand years ago? If we agree with the campaign literature of Amnesty International that capital punishment is not a punishment but a crime, then why did Jesus *have to* die? Should there not be an agreement between the theological accounts of the death of Jesus and legal reasoning, especially when considering the death penalty?

God's Nature and Grace Revealed in a Poor Person's Offering

In Hebrews 9:22 it is written, "without the shedding of blood there is no forgiveness of sins." Is this not clear proof that Jesus had to die, because his blood *had to* be shed—and does this not have consequences for how we view capital punishment today?[6] In other words, how are we to understand this statement in the Epistle to the Hebrews?

First of all, of course, we must read the entire verse from the beginning. Here is the text as written in the New Revised Standard Version of the Bible: "Indeed, under the law almost everything is purified with blood, and without the shedding of blood there is no forgiveness of sins." Four particularly important words can be noted in the Greek text: *schedon . . . kata ton nomon* (almost [everything] . . . under the law). Blood is *not* unconditionally necessary for reconciliation under the law, according to this verse. Blood sacrifice may be the *usual* sacrifice, but it is not an irrefutable *requirement* for reconciliation. The expression "under the law" should be interpreted descriptively, not prescriptively as a command. The word "almost" also has meaning here. In other words, this is a *description* of the ritual in the Pentateuch, the first five books of the Hebrew Bible, not a universal *condition* that describes and delimits God.[7]

The most obvious case is in the instructions on sin offerings in Leviticus. "Speak to the people of Israel, saying: When anyone sins unintentionally in any of the LORD's commandments about things not to be done,

5. Acts 5:39.

6. For more about the ritual function of blood in Hittite texts and the Bible, see Feder, *Blood Expiation*.

7. Belousek, *Atonement*, 208.

and does any one of them: . . ."[8] A description follows of what the person who has sinned—unintentionally—must do. A person who cannot afford a sheep is allowed to offer God "two turtledoves or two pigeons, one for a sin offering and the other for a burnt offering."[9] Already we can observe the principle of making the sacrifice proportionate not to the sin *but to the financial situation of the person making the sacrifice.* What should a person who cannot even afford a pair of sacrificial doves do? The following words are particularly interesting and highly relevant in this context.

> But if you cannot afford two turtledoves or two pigeons, you shall bring as your offering for the sin that you have committed one-tenth of an ephah of choice flour for a sin offering; . . . Thus the priest shall make atonement on your behalf for whichever of these sins you have committed, and you shall be forgiven.[10]

In other words, the poorest of the poor—people who could not even afford to sacrifice a pair of doves—are instead called upon to sacrifice a small amount of flour. The proportions that are described have nothing to do with how severe the crime is, but rather with the individual's ability. Even the poorest of poor people could be reconciled and see their lives renewed. As Belousek correctly observes, this is an exception to the rule, but it is an exception that reveals how the nature and grace of God is expressed in the sacrificial system.[11] Two aspects of the sacrificial system must often be highlighted. First, the person with the most rules to follow was the high priest (the one highest in the hierarchy), and second, the poorest of the poor people (at the bottom of social hierarchy) were included in the care and grace of God.[12] We may conclude from this brief analysis of scripture that blood is *not* required for reconciliation. "Thus the priest shall make atonement on your behalf for whichever of these sins you have [unintentionally] committed, and you shall be forgiven."[13] The message is thus that God forgives regardless of people's financial ability. In sum, the foundation upon which reconciliation and forgiveness rest is

8. Lev 4:2.

9. Lev 5:7.

10. Lev 5:11–13. One tenth of an ephah is probably approximately 3.6 liters, or about 4 quarts, but could be as little as 2 quarts.

11. Belousek, *Atonement*, 194.

12. Fredriksen, "Did Jesus Oppose," 23 and Belousek, *Atonement*, 388.

13. Lev 5:13. Cf. vv. 6 and 10.

that God is God and humans are humans. God wants reconciliation—and humans need forgiveness.

Not all offerings were blood sacrifices, not all blood sacrifices were about sin, and a committed sin did not always necessitate that a blood sacrifice be made.[14] This investigation has found that the point is not to make an offering *instead of* something else or *at the expense of* something else; rather, the purpose is to offer a sacrifice *as a tangible expression* of something essential, a *manifestation* of something inevitable. The concept may seem remote today, yet it is an inevitable insight into the sacrificial world and era: *sacrifice was an expression of loyalty to the covenant, not an exception or a rebellion against it.*

When the offering ritual has been followed and the ceremony completed, God is satisfied—not because divine wrath has been averted, but because a believer has obeyed the command. There is no contrast between inner and outer beliefs; rather, outer behavior is a manifestation of an inner understanding. The point is to underscore that an offering may never serve as a replacement for devotion, righteousness, and justice.[15]

Nothing could be more misdirected than to claim that, in the Bible, the grace and forgiveness of God is automatically acquired through bloody animal sacrifices. This is proved in the exception of exceptions for the poorest of the poor. The exception for poor people is to include them, not exclude them. Devotion and confession are what is important, not the kind and size of offering.

Same Message in Galilee and on Golgotha?

The literature on the ethical principles of the Sermon on the Mount in the fifth, sixth, and seventh chapters of Matthew is so extensive as to be more or less insurmountable.[16] The purpose of this section is not to try to contribute to that specific debate; rather, the purpose here and now is more modest yet important, namely, to *investigate the similarities between*

14. It is also essential to recall the distinction between ritual and moral impurity. Offering in connection with the birth of a child, for example, was not motivated by a sin having been committed; the issue was not a crime against the rules of the covenant but an expression of a functioning relationship.

15. Belousek cites the following Bible verses: Isa 1:10–20, Jer 7:21–23, Hos 6:6, Amos 5:21–24 and Mic 6:6–8; see *Atonement*, 182.

16. For commentary on the Matthean "antitheses" (which would be better called "hypertheses"), see Svartvik, *Bibeltolkningen*, 53–55.

the teachings of Jesus in the Sermon on the Mount and the accounts of Jesus' crucifixion on Golgotha.

One example is the section on how the commandment, "Love your neighbor" should be obeyed.[17] Who is really meant by the word "neighbor"? The all-embracing definition of neighbor is made by referring to nature, by asking who experiences sun and rain. What can we learn from this?

> For he makes his sun rise on the evil and [*also*] on the good,
> and sends rain on the righteous and [*also*] on the unrighteous.[18]

In the world of the Bible, people do not long for the sun but for the opposite. The merciless rays of the sun in Job represent the vulnerability and suffering of humans, "like a slave who longs for the shadow."[19] That the sun rises over evil people is not so strange—what is strange is that it rises as well over good people! That it rains on the unrighteous tells us that, just as the unrighteous are also granted the rain to survive in a Middle Eastern climate, so too should the commandment to love one's neighbor include even those whom we find unrighteous. This is an expression of the ethics of the Sermon on the Mount.

What ethics are expressed then on Golgotha? Michael J. Gorman argues that an essential New Testament concept is that the Christian ideal is not the world's way of judging, sentencing, and condemning. Instead, it is ethics and theology that adhere to the cross. The way of the cross is the royal road. He calls it *cruciformity* (like the cross) as opposed to *cosmoformity* (like the world).[20]

We find these cruciform ethics in the Sermon on the Mount, but do we find the ethics of the Sermon on the Mount also on Golgotha? The theology of the cross should underscore that the cross is a revelation: Golgotha tells us *what* God is, *where* God is, and *who* God is.

Yet the way people think and speak of the justice of God was not changed by the cross, but remains worldly—this is the real obstacle, "the scandal." Paul used the Greek word *skandalon*. "Do not be conformed to this world, but be

17. Lev 19:18 is expanded upon in Matt 5:43–47.

18. Matt 5:45. For rabbinical parallels to the belief that God is also good to evil people, see e.g., Davies and Allison, *Gospel according to Saint Matthew*, 1.556.

19. Job 7:2.

20. Gorman, *Inhabiting*, 27: "kenosis—specifically cruciform kenosis, or cruciformity—is the essential attribute of God." See also Svartvik, *Förundran*, 79–84.

transformed by the renewing of your minds, so that you may discern what is the will of God—what is good and acceptable and perfect."[21]

The comparison need not be limited to the Sermon on the Mount. Similar principles can be found in the parables Jesus used. In his teaching, Jesus often mentions forgiveness, and in his parables he describes people who are granted things.[22] In his teaching, in his life, and even—but not only—in his death, he was the "author of life."[23]

One example occurs in the closing words of the story of the landlord paying laborers in his vineyard: "Am I not allowed to do what I choose with what belongs to me? Or are you envious because I am generous?"[24] What if we were to keep this in mind when we read and publish texts about the death of Jesus on the cross? Is it not odd, really, how often the death of Jesus on Golgotha is expressed as if it had to happen, because "God's justice *demands* it," and "God's holiness *requires* it," while the teachings in Galilee at the Mount of Beatitudes can be summarized with the well-known expressions, "turn the other cheek also," "go also the second mile," and "love your neighbor as yourself"?[25] How is it possible that we so often interpret and apply the messages from the two mounts in such different ways? What happens if we strive to find words for the events of the crucifixion in light of the Sermon on the Mount?

21. Rom 12:2. See Belousek, *Atonement*, 389: "This is the real scandal—the stumbling block—of the cross for most Christians: our thinking about God's justice has not been transformed by the cross but remains 'conformed to this world,' shaped by the scheme of this age (Rom 12:2)." The noun *skandalon* and the verb *skandalizein* appear a total of forty-four times in the New Testament.

22. See especially Matt 18:21–34. For further comments, see Svartvik, *Bibeltolkningen*, 191–92.

23. Acts 3:15. The Greek *ho archēgos tēs zōēs* can also be translated "trailblazer," "pioneer," or "captain."

24. Matt 20:15.

25. See Belousek, *Atonement*, 32. There is a striking discrepancy between traditional Christian teaching about Jesus' life and work and traditional Christian teaching about his death. Belousek argues that Jesus acted, lived, and died on Golgotha as he taught on the Sermon on the Mount (ibid., 36–37). He practiced on the cross what he preached on the Mount of Beatitudes. The crucifixion can be analyzed as a revelation of the ethics described in the Sermon on the Mount.

Espouse or Oppose Violence?

Might a comparison of the Sermon on the Mount and the execution mount, Golgotha, bring us to terms with the belief of those times—and our times, in many parts of the world—that absolute justice can only be administered through torture and the death penalty? Coming to terms means recognizing that the fundamental issue is our desire to torture and kill—in the name of justice. The challenge is to present the crucifixion in a way that neither *sanctions violence* nor *romanticizes suffering.* Can the words of the New Testament help Christians interpret the death of Jesus in a way that allows them to vanquish violence without sanctifying it?

It comes down to two different theologies about the crucifixion. Do God and God's will triumph *because of* violence, or do they triumph *in spite of* the violence? Should we *espouse or oppose* the idea that violence is a necessary condition of the emancipation, rehabilitation, and dignity of human beings? If we speak of the crucifixion as a revelation, then retribution in the form of torture and death is *not* a manifestation of *what, where, or who* God is.[26]

In this way, the cross becomes a means of deliverance—not from a holy wrath that demands compensation, but rather as an emancipatory insight that God acts independently and freely to free the world through Christ because of and through his faith and love for creation and everything God has created. The true stumbling block is not God's righteousness, but rather God's *grace.*[27] Belousek observes that the message in the Bible is that God does *not* want humans to die. God does not even wish death upon those who do evil. "As I live, says the Lord God, I have no pleasure in the death of the wicked, but that the wicked turn from their ways and live."[28] Why then would God desire the death of the most righteous, that is, of Jesus Christ?

> What God puts to death at the cross is not Jesus himself but the law of retribution—"the law of eternal consequences"—which demands that humanity be punished with death to pay for the crime of murdering Jesus (Col 2:13–14). That is, *God does not sacrifice Christ through the cross for the sake of satisfying the law of retribution, but rather God sacrifices the law of retribution through the cross of Christ for the sake of redeeming humanity.* . . . What the

26. Belousek, *Atonement*, 391.

27. See Belousek, *Atonement*, 389, 394, and 609.

28. Ezek 33:11, cf. 18:23. See also Belousek *Atonement*, 227.

> cross of Christ scandalously reveals, however, is that retribution is not near the heart of God.[29]

Mark Heim advocates for a similar interpretation. He says that the cross should be presented as coming to terms with the traditional way *humans* think.

> God is not just feeding a better and bigger victim into this machinery to get a bigger payoff, as the theory of substitutionary atonement might seem to suggest. . . . Jesus didn't volunteer to get into God's justice machine. God volunteered to get into ours.[30]

Yes, in sum, the cross can be described as a *skandalon;* however, we are making a fundamental mistake if we believe the people of antiquity were shocked to think a crime might be punishable by death. Rather, it is the opposite. The true stumbling stone, the theological "scandal," is the thought that God's true nature is *not* identical with the Roman Empire's way of executing prisoners in a cruel and painful crucifixion.

"For violence is not an attribute of God."

One of the earliest Christian writings goes under the name of the Epistle of Mathetes to Diognetus. Unfortunately, we are not familiar with the context of this letter, addressed to Diognetus. The fact is, not even the writing remains. The text, which was found by chance in 1436 by Thomas d'Arezzo in a fish store in Constantinople, was sadly destroyed in 1870 during the Franco-Prussian war. Fortunately, the epistle had already been copied. Without knowing the context of the epistle or having the original text, it is notoriously difficult to date. It is part of the collection of texts known as the Apostolic Fathers, but it may have been written as late as the 300s. If Hippolytus of Rome wrote the last two chapters, they must have been written in 235 at the latest. Paul Foster suggests that the epistle is written after 150 CE. It makes sense to date it to the second century because it fits the discourse of the Christian apologetics of the time. Diognetus may be the real recipient of the epistle, or the name could be an epithet (approximately "born of Zeus").[31] As already mentioned, we know little of the context in which the

29. Belousek, *Atonement*, 391.

30. Heim, "Saved," 218.

31. For the suggestion of Zeus, see *De apostoliska fäderna*, 208. For more on the fascinating history of the text, see Paul Foster, "Epistle to Diognetus." For a discussion of the

epistle was written. Its content is highly relevant to this context, however, especially the Christological presentation in the seventh chapter. The author appears convinced that Christology should not be expressed in ways that people normally think, speak, and act. Rather, it should be expressed in a different way, which we will call the cruciform approach.

> But in truth the Almighty and all-creating and invisible God himself founded among men the truth from heaven, and the holy and incomprehensible word, and established it in their hearts, not, as one might suppose, by sending some minister to men, or an angel, or ruler, or one of those who direct earthly things, or one of those who are entrusted with the dispensations in heaven, but the very artificer and Creator of the universe himself, by whom he made the heavens, by whom he enclosed the sea in its own bounds, whose mysteries all the elements guard faithfully; from whom the sun received the measure of the courses of the day, to whose command the moon is obedient to give light by night, whom the stars obey, following the course of the moon, by whom all things were ordered, and ordained, and placed in subjection, the heavens and the things in the heavens, the earth and the things in the earth, the sea and the things in the sea, fire, air, abyss, the things in the heights, the things in the depths, the things between them—him he sent to them. Yes, but did he send him, as a man might suppose, in sovereignty and fear and terror? Not so, but in gentleness and meekness, as a king sending a son, he sent him as King, he sent him as God, he sent him as Man to men, he was saving and persuading when he sent him, not compelling, for [violence] is not an attribute of God. (Greek *Bia gar ou prosesti tō[i] Theō[i].*) When he sent him he was calling, not pursuing; when he sent him he was loving, not judging.[32]

---

possible time frame, see ibid., 167. See also Meecham, *Epistle to Diognetus* and Marrou, *Diognète.*

32. Diogn. 7.3–5. The handwriting of the text that follows is incomplete, a *lacuna*, and thus difficult to interpret. Yet it seems the author intends to say that the day of final judgment will be violent. Typically found in the apologetic presentations of that—and this—time, is an anti-Jewish theology. The Epistle to Diognetus is no exception. See especially 3–4. The question can and should be asked: What is intended with the way in which *bia gar ou prosesti tō[i] Teō[i]* is expressed? When *bia* is used in Acts it often refers to violent events (e.g., Acts 5:26 "but without violence," 21:35 "the violence of the mob was so great," and 27:41 "the stern was being broken up by the force of the waves"). But on the other hand, the verb *biazein* is used in Matt 11:12 to describe how the kingdom of heaven arrives by force—or what is meant by "has suffered violence"? Could it be that "violence" is too strong a word and "force" too weak?" Could there be a third word? Lake's translation ("compulsion is not an attribute of God") has been modified: "violence is not an attribute of God."

Even in translation, the elegant style of the writing is apparent. The closing lines, especially, are relevant here. According to the author of the epistle, Christology cannot be expressed "as we humans would think" (Greek *hōs anthrōpōn an tis logisaito*). Human beings take for granted that God approaches them "to establish a reign of terror of dangers and fear." But God is different. That is not at all the way it is (Greek *ou men oun*) from a divine perspective. "For violence is not an attribute of God." This is an early example of a cruciform theology that emphasizes that the life and teachings of Jesus should not be proclaimed in a way that glorifies or defends divinely sanctioned violence.[33] The main point, nonetheless, is that when God and humans meet, it is not in ways and on conditions set by humans. *In all cases, the Epistle to Diognetus questions the belief that what God does for the good of people—for our "salvation," to use the traditional word—requires violence.*

We can conclude that the crucifixion is not the definitive confirmation and proof of the validity of punishment and retribution. Indeed, is not the opposite true? When crucifixion theology and the life of Jesus are not isolated from his teaching, it becomes clear that the cross is not the ultimate expression of divine retribution.[34]

This chapter has shown that when theology began to emphasize torture and death as necessary conditions for the grace and goodness of God, a change followed. Another, older perspective claims there is a different kind of change, a transformation that is not conditioned upon violence.

May It Be My Will That My Mercy May Subdue My Wrath

One of the many fascinating discussions in the Talmud is on the question of whether God prays. If God were to pray, how would God's prayer be formulated? The Talmudic discussion proposes it might go like this: "May it be my will that my mercy may subdue my wrath."[35] This is not *imitatio Dei* (to imitate God) but rather *imitatio hominum* (to imitate humans), a theology that uses the words and feelings of humans to discuss God—ultimately the task of all theology (meaning, more or less, "words about God").

33. Schrenk, "*biazomai*," *Theological Dictionary*, 1.609–13.

34. Cf. Belousek, *Atonement*, 25: "This popular doctrine sees the cross as the ultimate satisfaction of divine retribution: by his death, Jesus pays God the penalty due for humanity's sin to appease God's wrath so that God and humanity may be at peace."

35. *Talmud Bavli Berakhot* 7a.

The prayer of God, as described in the Talmud, refers to the two scales representing the fundamental divine dialectic in rabbinical Judaism between justice (Hebrew *din*) and mercy (Hebrew *rachamim*), weighing punishment versus good.[36] The Jewish tradition also includes discussions of the two ways to name God in the Bible: *Elohim* (often translated to "God") is one way; the other way is the tetragrammaton, from the Greek meaning that it consists of four letters, of the four Hebrew letters commonly transliterated into Latin letters as YHWH. In the Jewish tradition, they are rarely written and never spoken.[37] *Elohim* corresponds to *middat ha-din* (God as the God of justice). The tetragrammaton is a synonym of *middat rachamim* (God as the God of mercy and forgiveness). *Elohim* is a term for God, a way to refer to God, but the tetragrammaton *is* the name of God; it says something about who God *truly* is. A similar dialectic exists in the Christian tradition. In James's epistle, for example, we find the expression "mercy triumphs over judgment."[38]

Is this theology of reconciliation and redemption expressed in Christian liturgy? It is articulated in the traditional Christian devotion to Mary, mother of mercy, who prays for humanity. *Sancta Maria, mater Dei: ora pro nobis peccatoribus* (Holy Mary, Mother of God, pray for us sinners). In the oldest recorded prayer to Mary, possibly from as early as the 200s, we find the idea of people seeking protection from the one who represents *eusplagchnia* (mercy).

> In your mercy
> we seek shelter, Mother of God.
> Turn not from our prayers in our time of need
> and save us from danger,
> you the only pure, only blessed.[39]

36. E.g, *Mekilta De-Rabbi Ishmael, Shirata* 3 (2.28). See also Ljungman, *Guds barmhärtighet.*

37. Required reading for anyone who wants to know about the reverence and respect shown the tetragrammaton is the article by van Wijk-Bos, "Writing on the Water."

38. Jas 2:13: "For judgment will be without mercy to anyone who has shown no mercy; *mercy triumphs over judgment* (Greek *katakauchatai eleos kriseōs*)" (italics added). A discrepancy in word choice can be noted between verses 12 and 13. There may be reason to assume that verse 13 is a word-for-word reference to a previously known and acknowledged statement, e.g., Dibelius, *James*, 147–48.

39. Latin *sub tuam misericordiam.* Clearly, it is impossible in only a few lines to justly treat Mariology, the study of Jesus' mother, Mary. For further comments, see, for example, Stacpoole, ed., *Mary in Doctrine*; Pelikan, *Mary through the Centuries*; Cunneen, *In Search of Mary*; Brodd and Härdelin, eds., *Maria i Sverige*; McKnight, *Real Mary*; Guroian, *Melody*, 65–92; and Siri, *Walking with Mary.* Yet a brief review of the development

The common Christian tradition of closing prayer "in Jesus' name," or "through Jesus Christ, our Lord," expresses a similar concept: the person praying turns to God with the courage granted by faith in Christ. Again, an example of the dialectic between God's judgment and God's mercy. The honest and self-critical person constantly experiences limitations, weakness, vulnerability, and sinfulness (to name a few of the many words we use to describe our shortcomings). Yet there is comfort to be found in the one who is "the Father of mercies and the God of all consolation."[40] There is good reason to claim that this dialectic is fundamental and of crucial import for both Jews and Christians.

We now have three—brief—models of a dialectic between divine justice and divine mercy: first, the rabbinical concept of a scale for justice and for mercy; next, the trusting prayer devoted to Mary, *Theotokos* (Mother of God); and, finally, the shared faith that Christians come to the Father through the Son.[41] It is not the divine dialectic in and of itself we are examining here but rather the specific assumption that *violence* is needed to influence God.

---

of Mariology reveals that some Christians tend to be interested in Mary either excessively from a gynecological standpoint or not at all. The starting point of Mariological reflection should instead be Heb 4:15, which is about how Jesus is, "tested as we are, yet without sin" (Greek *kata panta kath' homoiotēta chōris hamartias*): Jesus, a human being, born of Mary ("as we are"), yet divine, born of the Father ("without sin").

40. 2 Cor 1:3.

41. Cf. John 14:6: "No one comes to the Father except through me." Much can be said about this statement, which must be the most quoted Bible verse in discussions about the theology of religions. In short, it should be pointed out that it is not possible to equate Jesus, Christ, the Son, and the Word. For Christians, Jesus is more than that historical person, Jesus from Nazareth, because he is also Christ (Greek *ho Christos),* but he was also more than Christ because, in Christian trinitarian reflection, he is the Son. Christian Christology is something more—or rather, *something other*—than Jewish messianism, though Daniel Boyarin recently has pointed out that there are greater similarities than scholars have previously argued. See *Jewish Gospels*. In the Gospel according to John, it is the Word (Greek *ho logos*), the divine voice, that speaks to humanity. Anyone desiring to take seriously the theology in John should read John 14:6 in light of the prologue (John 1:1–18) and then keep in mind that the meaning of the verse is that the divine Word makes it possible to listen to the Father. See Cobb, ed., *Christian Faith*, 12. Note, too, that in Johannine theology there is a complementary, nearly inverted, reasoning (John 6:44): "No one can come to me [the Son] unless drawn by the Father who sent me; and I will raise that person up on the last day."

Transaction or Transformation?

In the second chapter, on Christian preunderstandings of atonement, a deeply problematic interpretation of the events of Good Friday was briefly sketched: the Father punishes the Son, that the Son may thus appease the Father and thereby avert the divine wrath and the divinely meted death penalty. This viewpoint expresses a belief that a violent transaction takes place within the essential nature of God.[42] Yet this kind of internal accounting in violence is poorly supported in the Bible and fails to convince the people of today, who—ironically—live in a time when financial terms seem to be on everyone's lips. The events of Holy Week and the Christian Easter message cannot be reduced to a financial transaction transferring divine assets to a debit account in the balance sheet through Jesus' suffering. Almost two hundred years ago, Edward Irving coined the expression "stock-exchange divinity" to describe this theological model.[43] This kind of imagery fails to deliver justice to the bounty of grace expressed in the Bible and the early Christian tradition. The subject is not financial management, but an existential metamorphosis; not a *transaction*, but a *transformation*.[44] Lars Thunberg differentiates between what he calls a "masochistic" view, or the concept of God becoming human in order to suffer on behalf of human beings, and the view of God becoming human to enable human beings to fulfill the purpose for which they were created.[45]

The *oikonomia* (Greek for "economy" or "management") that needs be articulated here has a considerably broader meaning. The church fathers understood the term as the action of God in, with, and for all of

42. See Belousek, *Atonement*, 293 and Brock and Parker, *Proverbs*, e.g., 25: "I could see that when theology presents Jesus' death as God's sacrifice of his beloved child for the sake of the world, it teaches that the highest love is sacrifice. To make sacrifice or to be sacrificed is virtuous and redemptive. But what if this is not true? What if nothing, or very little, is saved? What if the consequence of sacrifice is simply pain, the diminishment of life, fragmentation of the soul, abasement, shame? What if the severing of life is merely destructive of life and is not the path of love, courage, trust, and faith? What if the performance of sacrifice is a ritual in which some human beings bear loss and others are protected from accountability or moral expectation?"

43. Irving, *Collected Writings*, 5.506, cited in Gunton, *Actuality of Atonement*, 100 and 129. Cf. Garrett, *Stories*, 13: "God as cosmic banker."

44. Guroian, *Melody*, 53: "Salvation is not simply a forensic transaction that changes our *legal status* before God, but also a transformation of our *very being* that imparts to humankind a share in God's own Triune life."

45. Thunberg, *Gudomliga ekonomin*, 222.

creation, action that above all is characterized by God's grace: It is a divine, unbounded, and spontaneous initiative.[46] Gunton has commented on the theology of the Epistle to Diognetus as follows:

> Not here some grim balancing of accounts but rejoicing in a liberation. *The Son of God has given himself to be where we are so that we might be where he is, participants in the life of God.* And corresponding to that gift is the complete self-giving that is required, but likewise as a free and glad response. "I appeal to you therefore . . . to present your bodies as a living sacrifice, holy and acceptable to God" (Rom 12.1).[47]

The reasoning of several church fathers, including Athanasius of Alexandria (298–373) and Irenaeus (130–202), support the italicized section in the citation of Gunton: Christ became what we are so that we might become what he is.[48] *This* kind of transaction, between the divine and the human, is referred to in early Christian literature. The oldest explicit evidence of this line of thought can be found in the words of the New Testament: "Thus he has given us, through these things, his precious and very great promises, so that through them you may escape from the corruption that is in the world because of lust and may become *participants of the divine nature* (Greek *genēsthe theias koinōnoi fuseōs*)."[49]

In later interpretations, however, two things happened. First came the idea that God demanded *violence* in the form of a bloody sacrifice to appease the divine wrath. A recurring concept in Belousek's book on atonement, justice, and peace is that the argumentation in the New Testament is

46. The word *oikonomia* has different meanings in the New Testament. In one of Jesus' similes, he refers to the accounting of a manager (Luke 16:2), and Paul uses the term as a commission (1 Cor 9:17). Only later is the concept used as the church fathers would come to use it (Eph 1:10; 3:2, 9; and 1 Tim 1:4), namely, to describe God's actions in, with, and for creation, e.g., Gunton, *Actuality of Atonement*, 165: "the gracious initiative of God in re-creation." An indication that *oikonomia* is not limited to the crucifixion is the important role conferred upon Jesus' mother Mary in *to mysterion tēs oikonomias* (God's] unfathomable actions [with humankind]); see, Pelikan, *Mary through the Centuries*, 56–57, 103–4 and 212–13.

47. Gunton, *Actuality of Atonement*, 140 (italics added). Cf. the theology of surprise—as opposed to that of the logically necessary—in the Epistle to Diognetus 9.5: "O, what an *unfathomable* (Greek *anexichniastou*) creation, O, what a *surprising* (Greek *aprosdokētōn*) benefaction!" (italics added).

48. For reference, see Lossky, *Mystical Theology*, 134.

49. 2 Pet 1:4 (italics added). This concept will be further developed in chapter 9.

not that God is acting *against* Christ, but *with* and *through* him. God does not act *against* Christ but *for* the world and *for* humanity.[50]

Second came a shift in perspective by describing God as the *object* in the atonement process. In the previous chapter, we learned that the concept of reconciliation in the Hebrew Bible was that neither humans nor God were the objects of the verb *le-khapper* (to atone) in the instructions on sacrifice. Yet God is active in the process.[51] Reconciliation is an act of God within the terms of the covenant with humanity. It must be emphasized that, where the death of Jesus is interpreted using Jewish sacrificial terminology and theology, God is the *subject*, not the object. It is God who is active in the ritual and therefore in the process.[52]

> Sacrifice is God's way of making atonement. In atoning sacrifice, God is the primary actor, not humans; sacrifice atones, not because it "satisfies" God, but because God acts thorough [*sic*] it to make atonement.[53]

In this section we have examined the fundamental dialectic between God's judgment and mercy—and even between human brokenness and need for forgiveness. It has given rise to a way of speaking about the theology of the cross by using financial terminology, as an internal transaction of the divine Trinity. However, this approach has little support in early Christian literature. Rather, we find, in the New Testament and among the church fathers, a way of discussing the crucifixion as an *oikonomia,* which is a way to describe the spontaneous, life-giving, merciful, abundant generosity found in both God's creation and God's salvation. A love, in the words of Carl-Johan Vallgren,

> as great as that the Creator felt for his Creation, for human beings, beyond their sins and virtues, a love that existed in and of

50. In Rom 5:8, we should recall, "But God proves his love for us in that while we still were sinners Christ died for (Greek *hyper)* us." To do something *for* someone is not the same thing as doing *it instead of* someone else.

51. Fredriksen, *Jesus of Nazareth*, 69. If we are to use the theologically charged terms "object" and "subject," then God should be called the subject, that is, the one performing the action of the verb. Yet the ambition of this book lies beyond this distinction of objective and subjective atonement doctrine, which may be well established but is nonetheless limited and limiting. It does not do justice to the multifaceted texts of the Bible.

52. Belousek, *Atonement*, 188–91, 294 and 311.

53. Belousek, *Atonement*, 190–91.

> itself, that would hold together Creation, so the universe would not lose its meaning.[54]

The main purpose of this chapter has been to show that it is not the dialectic itself that is problematic, but rather the *assumption that violence is necessary to appease the wrath of God.* In other settings we sometimes say that "violence begets violence." Could it truly be so different when speaking of the divine world and the values that might appease our God?

Two Drastic Images

The next two chapters are devoted to particularly violent metaphors of the New Testament. In the second chapter of the Epistle to the Ephesians, the work of Jesus is described as causing a dividing wall to crumble, and in three of the Gospels are descriptions of the temple veil being torn in connection with the death of Jesus. *How can we understand these two motifs, the torn-down dividing wall and the curtain rent in two?* What are these texts saying? We turn now to the Epistle to the Ephesians.

54. Vallgren, *Den vidunderliga kärleken*, 318.

6

Reinterpreting the Dividing Wall of Enmity

It is of utmost importance to be aware of two separate groups, Jewish Christians and gentile Christians, if we are to understand the context and issues of the earliest Christian theology. In other words, one group in the early Christian movement was made up of Jews who were familiar with scripture, probably had participated in synagogue services all their lives, and may have sacrificed in the temple of Jerusalem at the major holidays of Passover, Pentecost (the Feast of Weeks or the Feast of Fifty days), and Sukkot. The other group of Christians were gentiles, or non-Jews who had become interested in Jewish scripture, theological reasoning, and liturgy. Belief in Jesus was their path to the God of Israel. We can cite a well-known verse in the Bible to describe what these gentiles surely felt, which was that none of them would have come to the Father except through the Son.[1] *The path to God for gentile Christians was radically different from the path for Jewish Christians.* If we ignore this irrefutable fact, we will have difficulties comprehending some of the most fundamental motifs as understood and used in early Christian writings. No other text in the New Testament is likely to make this clearer than the second chapter of the Epistle to the Ephesians. Therefore, examining this epistle closely is our immediate task.

"So he came and proclaimed peace to you who were far off and peace to those who were near."

The second chapter in Ephesians is arguably the New Testament text that most explicitly uses spatial metaphors when describing how belief in Christ brings people closer to God. Those who once were far off are now brought near:

1. Cf. John 14:6: "No one comes to the Father except through me."

> So then, remember that at one time you Gentiles by birth, called "the uncircumcision" by those who are called "the circumcision"—a physical circumcision made in the flesh by human hands—remember that you were at that time without Christ, being aliens from the commonwealth of Israel, and strangers to the covenants of promise, having no hope and without God in the world. *But now in Christ Jesus you who once were far off have been brought near by the blood of Christ.* For he is our peace; in his flesh he has made both groups into one and has broken down the dividing wall, that is, the hostility between us. He has abolished the law with its commandments and ordinances, that he might create in himself one new humanity in place of the two, thus making peace, and might reconcile both groups to God in one body through the cross, thus putting to death that hostility through it. So he came and proclaimed peace to you who were far off and peace to those who were near; for through him both of us have access in one Spirit to the Father. So then you are no longer strangers and aliens, but you are citizens with the saints and also members of the household of God.[2]

This quotation reminds us that the fundamental perspective in the New Testament epistles, and not only in the epistles that are genuinely Pauline, is that the ministry, life, death, and resurrection of Jesus is the way God chose to make it possible for gentiles—that is, non-Jews—to come to God.

Today, when we use the Christian calendar in many parts of the world, it is easy to forget that when the New Testament was written, the situation was radically different. At that time there was a scattering of people who believed in Christ who gathered in communities where *Jewish* texts were read, *Jewish* terminology was used, and *Jewish* holidays may have been celebrated (though perhaps with renewed meaning).[3] The expressions "far off" and "near" were used in the Epistle to the Ephesians because *parts of the non-Jewish population were approaching the Jewish faith and the Jewish people.*[4] By reading from the Bible and using Jewish terminology, they asserted that God had appeared to the people of Israel in a historically unique way.

2. Eph 2:11–19 (italics added).

3. For a presentation of the rise of early Christianity, see Stark, *Rise of Christianity*. For the many ties between Jewish and Christian holidays, see Göran Larsson, *Tid för Gud*.

4. When reading Acts 26:26 we are reminded of the geographical and theological center and periphery: When Paul meets Agrippa he says: "Indeed the king knows about these things, and to him I speak freely; for I am certain that none of these things has escaped his notice, for this was not done in a corner" (Greek *ou gar estin en gōnia[i] pepragmenon touto).* On election, see Kaminsky, *Yet I Loved Jacob*.

> It was not because you were more numerous than any other people that the LORD set his heart on you and chose you—for you were the fewest of all peoples. It was because the LORD loved you and kept the oath that he swore to your ancestors, that the LORD has brought you out with a mighty hand, and redeemed you from the house of slavery, from the hand of Pharaoh king of Egypt.[5]

Today this perspective is sometimes dismissed as "tribalism" or "exclusivity," but it was most likely obvious to early Christians that the Christian faith had to do with the Jewish people, and that this people had long been in covenant with God. In sum, to approach the Jewish people was to approach the God of Israel, and to approach the God of Israel was to join with the Jewish people.

What Is the Dividing Wall, Really?

Primarily for its image of the torn-down dividing wall, the second chapter of Ephesians is the key text in this regard. It will now be discussed in greater depth. There are many reasons to believe that the epistle is primarily directed toward gentiles. This is the group described as, "you who once were far off have been brought near by the blood of Christ."[6] Most fascinatingly revealed here is the fundamental meaning of "offering" (Hebrew *qorban*). In antiquity, as Halbertal argues, offerings brought people closer to God. Likewise, Christ, according to New Testament theology, brings gentiles closer to God.

Now, what is meant by "the dividing wall" (*to mesotoichon tou phragmou)* in Ephesians 2:15? The traditional interpretations can be ordered in four main categories.

(a) The interpretation that is often put forth in commentary and analyses is that it represents the fence (*soreg*) in the temple of Jerusalem between the courtyard of the gentiles and the area of Israel. The Hebrew name for this separator is *ha-soreg.* It was a fence that was ten cubits high (approximately 80 cm).[7] If we believe that *to mesotoichon tou phragmou* in Ephesians refers

5. Deut 7:7–8.

6. Eph 2:13.

7. See *Mishnah Middot* 2.3: *liphnim mimmenu soreg gavoha ʿasarah tephachim* (On the inside [existed] a ten-cubit high fence). For more on this unit of measurement, see 1 Kgs 7:26 or Ezek 40:5 ("handbreadth"). According to Josephus, this fence was three cubits, approximately 1.3 meters, high.

to this *soreg*, we may need to find a better word than "dividing wall," because the word "wall" does not bring to mind a fence that is barely a meter tall.[8] An argument against this interpretation of *ha-soreg* is that the term is not used by the Jewish historian Josephus (37/38–100) when he describes the temple in Jerusalem.[9] A counterargument, however, by Martin Kitchen points out that it can hardly be viewed as a technical term.

According to this first interpretation, "the dividing wall" is not strictly a metaphor but a reference to an actual, physical fence. If Ephesians is a deuteropauline epistle (which would mean it is not written by Paul, but perhaps by one of his disciples) it may have been written after the fall of the temple in 70, making it highly relevant in this context.[10] Could the author mean that the boundary between Jews and non-Jews was abolished after the destruction of the temple? That Paul brought Greeks (in other words, non-Jews) to Jerusalem is mentioned relatively often in the twenty-second chapter of Acts of the Apostles. But in the preceding chapter it is actually written that people "had previously seen Trophimus the Ephesian with him in the city, and *they supposed that* Paul had brought him into the temple."[11] It is not written that Paul actually did it. On the contrary, in a previous verse, the opposite is stated. "Thus all will know that there is *nothing* in what they have been told about you, *but that you yourself observe and guard the law.*"[12] It could be a diversion to suggest that the author of Acts claims Paul intentionally defied the rules of the temple of Jerusalem. But could it be that the author of Ephesians, who wrote the epistle several decades after Paul's epistles surfaced, interpreted the mission among the gentiles in light of the fall of the temple? Could it be a way to give theological meaning to the historical catastrophe, not in a triumphalist way, but in a conciliatory and transforming way?

(b) A more specific interpretation is that the dividing wall refers to a notion we find in the rabbinic literature that there is a need for "a fence

8. For additional comments, see *History of the Jewish People*, 2.285 n.57; Best, *Commentary on Ephesians*, 250–59; and Branham "Penetrating the Sacred," especially 12–16.

9. The Greek expressions are *herkion lithinou druphaktou, druphaktos peribeblēto lithinos* or *ho druphaktos;* see *Antiquitates Judaicae* 15.416–17, and *Bellum Judaicum* 5.193 and 6.124–25. For more on Josephus, see Lycke, *Flavius Josephus* and Raphael, *Jew among Romans*.

10. For a summary of arguments for a deuteropauline authorship, see Kitchen, *Ephesians*, 4–7. For a thorough discussion, see Mitton, *Epistle to the Ephesians*.

11. Acts 21:29 (italics added).

12. Acts 21:24 (italics added).

around the Torah" (Hebrew *seyag la-Torah*).[13] Is the author of the Epistle to the Ephesians objecting to the growing attempts of the rabbinical movement to extend the application of the *mitswot?* The rabbinical expression *seyag la-Torah* is unfortunately often misunderstood by Christians. This is actually rather curious, as much of the teaching in the Sermon on the Mount could be described as *seyag la-Torah*, that is, an attempt to interpret the *mitswot* maximalistically, such as applying the command not to kill *also* to those who are angry at and therefore insult a brother or sister. Or, extending the commandment not to commit adultery *also* to those who look at other persons with lust.[14] It is difficult to avoid the feeling that this second interpretation stems from an anachronistic view. On the one hand, the concept of *seyag la-Torah* may not yet have become a known and accepted term; on the other hand, what may be the oldest reference to it can be found in the holy scripture of Christianity, the New Testament. The argument that the author of the Epistle to the Ephesians would object specifically to *seyag la-Torah* is unconvincing.

(c) A third possibility is that it refers to an ontological dividing wall between heaven and earth, between the eternal and temporal worlds, between God and humanity.[15] This interpretation raises a number of questions. Can it be that nothing separates heaven and earth from each other following the life, death, and resurrection of Jesus?[16] In other words, could the author possibly believe it had not been previously possible to approach God, that there existed no relationship with God in the time of the Hebrew Bible? Is the author saying that the psalmists wrote and sang without any theological knowledge or sense of who God is? That the prophets did not speak on behalf of God? All these questions indicate that this simply is not a convincing interpretation.

(d) The fourth interpretation combines the reference to the "dividing wall" with the reference to the law per se in the following paragraph. In other words, Christ's mission would have been to abolish Jewish law.[17]

13. See *Mishnah Pirqe Avot* 1.1.

14. Matt 5:17–48. A related question is whether the concept of *anti*theses is applicable here or whether the concept of *hyper*theses would be more appropriate. See Svartvik, *Bibeltolkningen*, 53–55.

15. 1 En. 14.9. See Kitchen, *Ephesians*, 65–66.

16. One is reminded of Christian presentations of texts on the rending of the temple veil in connection with the death of Jesus. See the discussion in the next chapter.

17. See Lincoln, *Ephesians*. (a) First Lincoln argues that Christ neutralized the negative effects of the law (142: "Christ neutralized these negative effects of the law by doing

This has been a particularly influential interpretation, not least in the Lutheran tradition. The ulterior—and problematic—reasoning is that the greatest mistake a person can make is to believe that the law can save a person, and that a person can be saved by obeying the law. One wonders, however, in what way this interpretation can be reconciled with the statement that the message is "peace for those who are near." If the law is the fundamental problem of humanity, and if Jesus came to abolish the law (and, thereby, Jewish faith and tradition), how could this possibly be conceived as a message of peace by Jews?[18] Nor would many Jews identify with the description of being "saved" by "observing the commandments." Jews who keep the laws in *ha-Torah* do so because God "has sanctified us with his commandments" (Hebrew *qiddeshanu be-mitswotaw*).[19] So this interpretation is also questionable.

Tet-Lim N. Yee offers a modification of the above view. He seems to say that *aspects* of the law that differentiated Jew from gentile no longer apply. He describes this use of law as a biblically motivated ethnic antagonism:

> What is at stake, however, is not the law *per se* but the law as the Jews had used it to consolidate their Jewish identity. . . . This, the enmity between Jew and Gentile, lies not with the Torah *per se* but with the human attitude that perverted the gifts of God into signs of separation and exclusiveness. However, the law . . . is now abolished through the death of Christ.[20]

Yee wrote his dissertation for Durham University, where James D. G. Dunn was active for many years. Dunn is one of the scholars who introduced the "New Perspective on Paul." Yee's book extensively expresses

---

away with the law"). (b) Then he claims that Christ abolished the law *per se* (142 and 144: "in order to remove the divisiveness Christ has to deal with its cause—the law itself. . . . In his death Christ abolished the law . . . and terminated the old order dominated by that law, which had prevented the Gentiles from having access to salvation. . . . The separation of the Gentiles from Israel and her election was a cleft so deep that it took the creative act of Christ's death to fill it"). (c) Finally he argues that the law was not favorable to Israel (146 and 163: "the law . . . separated Israel from God. . . . Israel too was alienated from her God").

18. See Bentzer, *Lagen och nåden*, 5: "The Epistle to the Galatians provides insight into the difficult battle already being fought by the young Christian church to assert the gospel's message of grace toward both gentile and Jewish religion. The epistle is short but intense. In condensed form it presents the incompatibility of the paths to salvation by the law versus grace."

19. See Scherman, *Complete ArtScroll Siddur*, 2.

20. Yee, *Jews, Gentiles and Ethnic*, 158 and 160–61.

Dunn's perspective on the writings and theology of Paul, namely that Paul objected to the way Jewish law put up boundaries that separated Jews from gentiles.[21] It is nonetheless difficult to avoid drawing the conclusion that Yee allows Jewish faith in the covenant to express a general phenomenon: every group identity creates some form of boundary to its surroundings. Yee concludes that the death of Jesus abolishes the Jewish commandments. Jewish faith in the commandments seems to him to be a problem to solve, not a life to live.

The Wall as a Metaphor

None of these four interpretations is convincing. How, then, should we understand "the dividing wall" discourse? The fifth and most persuasive interpretation is that the expression truly is a *metaphor*. Nelson Goodman has said that a metaphor is "teaching an old word new tricks."[22] The phrase "they cried rivers of tears" contains a metaphor (that is, "rivers of tears"). The statement, "The Nile is the world's longest river" does not, nor does the statement, "they shed many tears." "Complaints flood in" is a metaphor, but neither the word "complaint" nor "flood" is. If the Greek expression *to mesotoichon tou phragmou* were simply a reference to the temple of Jerusalem, it would not be a metaphor. If it is an image, then it is a metaphor. If it refers to the things that truly divide people, namely mistrust, enmity, and hatred, then it is a metaphor. In fact, this was explicitly stated in the Epistle to the Ephesians. Enmity (Greek *hē echthra*) is the true dividing wall between individuals and peoples—and it is much higher than ten hands! The true dividing wall between people is not diversity but intolerance. The greatest obstacles to genuine understanding are not differences but schisms.

A question briefly touched upon above demands a more comprehensive response. What can it mean to state, "He has abolished the law and its commandments and ordinances?"[23] The answer to this question cannot possibly

21. Yee defended his dissertation in 1999. Dunn, "New Perspective on Paul." It should be noted that this "new" perspective is now over thirty years old. Other, newer perspectives exist. For the "radical new perspective" on Paul and his epistles, see Eisenbaum, *Paul Was Not a Christian*. For a summary of critical views on the new perspective, see Svartvik, "'East is East.'"

22. Goodman's expression cited in Gunton, *Actuality of Atonement*, 28.

23. Eph 2:15 (Greek *ton nomon tōn entolōn en dogmasin katargēsas*). The word *en dogmasin* ([and] in regulations) is lacking from p46, which is one of the oldest New Testament papyri, typically dated at 200 CE.

be that all scripture be negated. Early Christianity was not a lawless religion. Even the very first generation of Christians held ethical principles.[24] An explicit spatial metaphor must have been employed here to describe how some people were once far away from God. Truly, the problem could not have been that some people already were close to God.

Could it be that "the law with its commandments and ordinances" refers to *the commandments that apply only to Jews,* in other words, the ordinances that theologically excluded gentiles? The gentiles, having been brought near, were no longer excluded by the scripture. Through Jesus, the commandments that excluded gentiles could do so no longer, because God had opened a way "apart from law (Greek *chōris nomou*; or literally 'without law'), as attested by the law and the prophets."[25]

Obviously, the Greek words, translated as "dividing wall," are a metaphor. Important to note is that the author of the Epistle to the Ephesians emphasizes the *enmity* between people as the problem, not the destruction of the temple as a prerequisite for improved relations between Jews and non-Jews. Hatred between people is the underlying and encompassing problem. Therefore, assertions that spread contempt for other groups of people are deeply disturbing.

Nations Will Come to Your Light

Yee seems to take for granted that Jewish exclusivism is the problem, and that it must be broken down and abolished for there to be peace between those who are far off and those who are near. But can we truly assume that Jewish exclusivism is the problem? Is an alleged Jewish self-confidence the greatest challenge to the Christian faith? A renewed understanding of the second chapter in Ephesians is needed. An interesting yet rarely cited parallel is to be found in 2 Baruch. The author of the text is unknown. Writing under the pseudonym of Baruch, the author served as secretary to the prophet Jeremiah, thereby placing the writing of the text at the time of the destruction of the First Temple of Jerusalem, Solomon's Temple.[26] The next section is especially relevant here, as it reveals yet another possible interpretation of the text on the dividing wall in Ephesians.

24. See Paul's writing in 1 Cor 5:1–5 on a sexual relation that is forbidden in both Roman and Jewish law (Lev 18:8).

25. Rom 3:21.

26. The name Baruch is mentioned four times in Jeremiah (in Jer 32, 36, 43, and 45).

> He who reveals to those who fear him what awaits them, so that from here on he will console them, he makes known the mighty deeds to those who do not know—he breaks the barrier (Syriac *suga*) for those who are not persuaded and enlightens the darknesses and reveals what is hidden to those who are without blemish, those who have subjected themselves in faith to you and to your *Torah*.[27]

It is probable that 2 Baruch was written after the fall of the Second Temple in 70 CE: Albertus Frederik Johannes Klijn suggests that 2 Baruch was written down between 100 and 120 CE; Liv Ingeborg Lied argues that it came about one or two decades after year 70 CE; and Matthias Henze believes it was written down during the period between the two Jewish revolts against Rome, which would make it between the years 70 and 132.[28] In other words, if the Epistle to the Ephesians is deuteropauline, the two texts would have been written approximately during the same period. The source of the preserved Syriac handwritten document was probably a Hebrew original that was also the source of a paraphrased fragment in Greek found in Oxyrhynchus, Egypt.[29] Most scholars today believe the work to be a theological response to the destruction of the temple and as a deliberation on the situation of Jewish societies following that cataclysmic historical event.[30]

27. 2 Bar. 54.3–5. Many thanks to Liv Ingeborg Lied who provided translation and interpretation of this key text. Cf. translation by Stone and Henze, *4 Ezra*, 119: "He who reveals to those who fear him what awaits them, so that from here on he will console them, he makes known the mighty deeds to those who do not know—he breaks the barrier for those who are not persuaded, and enlightens the darknesses and reveals what is hidden to those who are without blemish, those who have subjected themselves in faith to you and to your Torah." See also A. F. J. Klijns older translation, "2 (Syriac Apocalypse of) Baruch," 639: "You are the one to whom both the depths and the heights come together, and whose Word the beginnings of the periods serve. You are the one who reveals to those who fear that which is prepared for them so that you may comfort them. You show your mighty works to those who do not know. You pull down the enclosure (Syriac *suga)* for those who have no experience and enlighten the darknesses, and reveal the secrets to those who are spotless, to those who subjected themselves to you and your *Torah* in faith." For the Syriac word that is key here, *suga* (obstacle); cf. Song 7:2: "Your navel is a rounded bowl that never lacks mixed wine. Your belly is a heap of wheat, encircled [Hebrew *suga*] with lilies."

28. Klijn, "2 (Syriac Apocalypse of) Baruch," 617, Lied, "Those Who Know," 427, and Stone and Henze, *4 Ezra*, 10.

29. Oxyrhynchus Papyrus 3.403 contains 2 Bar. 12.1—13.2 and 13.11—14.2.

30. See Lied, "Those Who Know," 427–28: "Most scholars today understand the work as a response to that destruction and as a deliberation over the situation of Jewish

What is so interesting is that the author of 2 Baruch writes of a dividing wall that has been torn down, but in this case, it is not an alleged Jewish exclusivism that is the problem (as Yee claims is the case in Ephesians); rather, it is people's lack of knowledge, which God will cure by revealing mighty deeds. "You pull down the enclosure *for those who have no experience and enlighten the darknesses*."[31] In other words, the problem is a theological exclusivity, not theological inclusivity. This motif appears in several texts, for example in Isaiah 25, as a sheet shrouding all the *non-Jewish* peoples, but that shall one day be destroyed.

> On this mountain the LORD of hosts will make for all peoples (*le-khol-ha-'ammim*) a feast of rich food, a feast of well-aged wines, of rich food filled with marrow, of well-aged wines strained clear. And he will destroy on this mountain the shroud that is cast over all peoples (*kol-ha-'ammim*), the sheet that is spread over all nations (*kol ha-goyim*).[32]

Yet again, it is a matter of the nations, the peoples, of the world gaining spiritual enlightenment, not of the Jewish people being destroyed.[33] *This appears as well in the nineteenth chapter of Isaiah.*

> On that day Israel will be the third (*shlishiyyah*, "a triad") with Egypt and Assyria, a blessing in the midst of the earth, whom the LORD of hosts has blessed, saying, Blessed be Egypt my people, and Assyria the work of my hands, and Israel my heritage.[34]

This perspective can be found yet again in sections of Isaiah that were written later, for example in the sixtieth chapter:

> Arise, shine; for your light has come, and the glory of the LORD has risen upon you. For darkness shall cover the earth, and thick darkness the peoples (Hebrew *le-ummim*); but the LORD will arise

---

societies following the loss of the temple" and Stone and Henze, *4 Ezra*, 10: "The author of *2 Baruch* wrote in response to the Roman destruction of Jerusalem in 70 CE, though the apocalypse is set factiously during and after the Babylonian sacking of Jerusalem in the year 587 BCE."

31. Italics added.

32. Isa 25:6–7. See also Zech 6:15: "Those who are far off shall come and help to build [i.e., not 'tear down'] the temple of the LORD."

33. Sommer, "Isaiah," 832: "When the new cosmic order emerges, the illusions that befuddle the nations will disappear, and the survivors from all nations will enjoy access to true teachings, which emanate from the God of Zion."

34. Isa 19:24.

> upon you, and his glory will appear over you. Nations (Hebrew *goyim*) shall come to your light, and kings to the brightness of your dawn. Lift up your eyes and look around; they all gather together, they come to you (*kulam niqbetsu vau lakh*); your sons shall come from far away (*banayikh merachoq yavou*), and your daughters shall be carried on their nurses' arms.[35]

The text in Isaiah that is most similar to the one in Ephesians, however, "Peace, peace, to the far and the near," can be found in the fifty-seventh chapter. "'Peace, peace, to the far and the near,' says the LORD."[36] In the Hebrew, the word "peace" is repeated: *shalom shalom la-rachoq we-la-qarov, amar Adonay* (literally, "Peace, peace, to the far and the near, says the LORD").[37] The message of peace thus applies to *both* those who were once far away *and* those who already were near.

In sum, the purpose of quoting all these writings—from 2 Baruch and from Isaiah—is to demonstrate an equally substantiated alternative to the traditional, triumphalist reading that simplistically maintains that Jewish life be declared null and void as a condition for good relations between Jews and non-Jews. Given the writings quoted, it seems much more probable that the intent was not to abolish Judaism but to bring closer those who used to be "far away" (cf. Hebrew *qorban*). This would abolish enmity and hostility (*hē echthra*). In short, it is not the already-gained theological insights of *Judaism* that is the theological problem, but the lack of knowledge of the *gentiles*. The point is not that a gentile Christian life is superior to a Jewish life, but that the gentiles through Christ have been granted a covenantal relationship similar to the one Israel already has.[38] There is good

35. Isa 60:1–4. The first words are part of the song *lekha dodi,* which is sung at the Jewish worship service *qabbalat shabbat* every Friday evening.

36. Isa 57:19. Isaiah 57:14—58:14 is currently *haphtarah* (that is, readings from the prophets) for Yom Kippur, the great Day of Atonement. The oldest evidence we can find of one of these *haphtarah* readings is actually in the New Testament in Luke 4:17 and Acts 13:15.

37. In the Septuagint, the Greek version of the Jewish scriptures, it reads *eirēnēn ep' eirēnēn tois makran kai tois engus ousin* (Peace beyond peace to those [who are] far away and to those who are near). In rabbinic hermeneutics we find the belief that there are no unnecessary words in the Torah. Anyone applying these hermeneutics would argue that the word *shalom* is repeated because the verse has a hidden meaning, perhaps that peace applies to those who are far away *as well as* to those who are near. The specific meaning of each word was emphasized especially by Rabbi 'Aqivah in, for example, Heschel, *Heavenly Torah*, 46–64.

38. Williamson and Allen, *Interpreting Difficult Texts*, 75.

reason to assume that "the law with its commandments and ordinances" does not refer to all Jewish writings or all Jewish traditions, but only the specific tradition of interpretation that argued that *only* Jews could have a covenantal relationship with God.

Who Really Is God's Israel?

There is a specific difficulty with the Epistle to the Ephesians: If this epistle is truly by Paul, then it can and should be read in light of his other epistles. If it is not, then we cannot draw parallels in the same way between the New Testament epistles. In New Testament research there is no consensus on the author of Ephesians. As a result, the new models of interpretation generally accepted in the study of the undisputed Pauline epistles have been less applied to Ephesians.[39] For just this reason, it may be valuable to compare it with an epistle that all researchers actually believe to be truly Pauline, namely the Epistle to the Galatians. In its last chapter, Paul writes in a similar manner. In the New Revised Standard Version of the Bible, the verse is translated as follows: "For neither circumcision nor uncircumcision is anything; but a new creation is everything! As for those who will follow this rule—peace be upon them, and mercy, and upon the Israel of God."[40] The translation is faithful to the Greek original, at the end of the last sentence, where it reads, *eirēnē ep' autous kai eleos kai epi ton Israēl tou Theou*, which is translated, "peace be upon them, and mercy, and upon the Israel of God," i.e., as two distinct groups. In the theology of Paul there is a clear message that *peace and mercy shall be shed upon both Jews and non-Jews*. The message is *not* that there no longer exists an Israel, or that there should not exist an Israel![41]

In Psalms, for example, we find wishes of peace upon Israel.[42] In the Epistle to the Galatians, Paul actually *extends* the wishes of peace to non-Jews. He does not *restrict* it, as some argue, by redefining "the Israel of God"

39. For a *new perspective* interpretation of the Epistle to the Ephesians, see however Weedman, "Reading Ephesians."

40. Gal 6:16. Yet in the Swedish Bible 2000, it is translated "åt dem som vill leva efter denna ordning, åt Guds Israel (upon them who will live by these rules, upon God's Israel)."

41. For further views, see Svartvik, "'East is East.'"

42. See Pss 125:5 and 128:6.

to refer to the church, thereby excluding Israel.[43] In short, it is not about uncircumcision being correct and circumcision being wrong, but that both can be right for different groups of people. The good news is not that Judaism and Jewish faith have been eliminated—for how could this be received as good news?—but that a covenant with God has been established to *include* those who do not belong to the people of Israel.

The dramatic change is that those who were far off (i.e., gentiles) have been brought close—not that those who were close (i.e., Jews) only believed they were, but actually were not, or that those who were close have now been driven far off. It is interesting to relate the spatial metaphors to the discourse of sacrifice as an act that brings humans *closer to God*—remembering that the author of the Epistle to the Ephesians writes that the gentiles have been brought near to God "by the blood of Christ." The ministry, life, death, and resurrection of Jesus is compared to the sacrifices in the temple, to that which, during the existence of the temple, brought people close to God. The theological exile of the gentiles has been replaced by the presence of Christ and a covenantal relationship. In the writing, they gain a theological citizenship. The author uses legal language ("citizens") to describe how the status of these gentiles has now changed from alienation to inclusion.

According to the author, gentiles have been brought near through Christ. The sacrificial discourse and the spatial metaphors ("far off" and "near") interrelate in a fascinating way. Jesus is the sacrifice in the sense that he brings gentiles closer to God. That is why the blood of Christ is specifically mentioned in this text. Jesus is like the sacrifice (the *qorban*) that brings the gentiles closer to God. But this does not imply that those who already were close now have been removed. The center of faith (God) has not been ejected from Israel; rather, those who had previously been in the periphery are injected. The Ephesians, gentile Christians far from the faith, are meant to realize that those who were far have been brought near God. This is the main point the author makes.

The recipients of the epistle are encouraged to no longer live as gentiles. "Now this I affirm and insist on in the Lord: you must no longer live as the Gentiles live."[44] In spite of this quite explicit appeal of the author, the epistle has oddly enough too often been understood as a call for Jews to no longer live as Jews! It is not an alleged Jewish exclusivism that separates Jew

43 See Stendahl, *Final Account*, 5 and 40; Eastman, "Israel and the Mercy of God."

44. Eph 4:17.

from non-Jew in Ephesians. No, *the epistle's good news is not that Jews have been disinherited but that the gentiles have become heirs with them.*

> That is, the Gentiles have become fellow heirs, members of the same body, and sharers in the promise in Christ Jesus through the gospel.[45]

An Interpretation of Reconciliation and Transformation

By way of summary, a closer analysis of the second chapter of Ephesians has been be fruitful for a number of reasons.

(a) The second chapter in Ephesians is the New Testament text that most explicitly uses *spatial metaphors* when describing how belief in Christ brings gentiles, who once were far off, near. The epistle is clearly directed primarily to gentile Christians (See Eph 4:17: "you must no longer live as the Gentiles live"). It is directed to those who were "aliens from the commonwealth of Israel, and strangers to the covenants of promise." That "now in Christ Jesus" they "who once were far off have been brought near" does not mean that everything God previously did for Israel and with Israel is abolished. The author of Ephesians writes of breaking down a dividing wall, obviously a metaphor for the enmity that actually separates people. It is a metaphor, a descriptive image.

(b) The author of the epistle uses *sacrificial terminology* to express how the ministry of Christ certainly includes those who are far away. Sacrifice is used as a concept because of the importance of the temple of Jerusalem, not because it was a theological obstacle or a manifestation of the enmity between God and humanity. By writing to the Ephesians and using the metaphor of the temple, the author of the epistle describes the mission to the gentiles. The gentiles, who had been far off, are brought near God through Christ. That is why "the blood of Christ" is mentioned in Ephesians 2:13. Not because God's sense of righteousness demands that blood be spilled, nor because the holy wrath of God inevitably leads to the violent death of Jesus. Rather, the author of the epistle chooses to use the metaphor of the temple to express the incorporation of the gentiles into the community of the covenant. The temple, for the author of Ephesians, is not a theological problem but a pedagogic metaphor.

45. Eph 3:6.

(c) The basis of the epistle is *not an antinomian theology* that rejects a socially established morality. The similarity to the quote from the second book of Baruch is striking. In that text, obedience to the *Torah* and grief at the fall of the temple are the obvious theological bases. The torn-down dividing wall is made of ignorance; the barrier is a lack of insight.

The division (that is, Jewish adherence to the covenant by *ha-Torah*) is no longer the only way to approach God, but it remains the theological alternative for Jews. "Here is neither Jew nor Greek" does not mean there no longer exists differences between Jews and non-Jews. The attitude of humans toward other humans is the problem, not that there exist other humans, or humans who are different. It is not the *differences* between people but rather the *discord* that must be opposed. In sum, the fundamental problem is not Jewish loyalty to the covenant but enmity among people, as the author of the epistle explicitly writes.

In this chapter we have seen that two early Christian groupings—Christian Jews and Christian gentiles—must be kept in mind in Christian theology. In Ephesians 2 it is written, "peace to you who were far off and peace to those who were near." We have found that the text about the torn-down dividing wall should not be understood as a rejection and even less as a condemnation of "those who were near," but instead an opportunity for those who previously had been "far off." When the dividing wall is gone, they can be included in the light of revelation. Their view had been previously obstructed by something that could be likened to a wall. The problem that is being described is the previous ignorance of the gentiles, not Jewish faith and life. *The conclusion we should draw is that a Christian theology of reconciliation and transformation that fails to take into account the unique position of Judaism before Christ can hardly be expected to respect it after Christ.*

But how, then, shall we understand New Testament writings of the temple veil being torn in connection with the death of Jesus? Might we read these texts and find the motif presented in a reconciling and transforming way? This will be the task of the next chapter.

7
Rendering the Rending of the Veil

Our task here will be to closely examine how Christians have interpreted the scriptures that describe how a curtain in the temple tore when Jesus died.[1] This great piece of fabric is usually called a veil.[2] The event took on crucial meaning as Christians began to formulate their theological responses to the death of Jesus. The Greek word *katapetasma* was used exclusively to refer to this curtain in Christian texts for several centuries, according to Daniel M. Gurtner.[3]

First, we should note that there is an impressive scholarly concord regarding this event. The vast majority of New Testament scholars argue that the verb form used, "was torn" (Greek *eschisthē*), should be read as a so-called divine passive (Latin *passivum divinum*).[4] In other words, this form, the divine passive, is used to indicate it is God who is the agent, that what is happening is a divine act. The same verb (Greek *schizein*) is used to describe what happens when Jesus is baptized by John in the Jordan river. Then the heavens "tore apart" (Greek *schizomenous*), and the Holy Spirit descended like a dove on Jesus.[5]

This *historical* event has demanded a *theological* interpretation.[6] The crucial question that follows is, how might these writings be interpreted?

1. Matt 27:51; Mark 15:38; and Luke 23:45. According to the descriptions in Matthew and Mark, the event occurs *after* the death of Jesus, and according to Luke, the curtain ruptures *before* Jesus' death.

2. A previous version of this chapter has been published in English in a *Festschrift;* see Svartvik, "Rendering." For an autobiographical approach, see Eskenazi, "With the Song."

3. Gurtner, *Torn Veil*, 76 n.19.

4. See Brown, *Death of the Messiah*, 2.1100.

5. Mark 1:10.

6. The focus here is not the question of whether it actually happened. Rather, the main question is the way in which the descriptions in the Synoptic Gospels have been interpreted.

The commentary on Matthew 27:51 in the Swedish Bible 2000 directs the reader's thoughts:

> A temple's inner room, the most holy, was separated by a curtain. Matthew clearly sees its rending as a sign that Jesus' death has opened the way to God.

However, this is not the only interpretation. How have readers of the Bible through the ages interpreted these texts, and how can they be interpreted today?[7] If there are more interpretations, why should we prefer some and not others? Is it possible to formulate the characteristic features of a good interpretation?

Donald A. Hagner argues that Matthew did not need to explain the event because everyone understood what the rending of the veil meant.[8] Raymond E. Brown maintains that neither Matthew nor his readers understand it.[9] As regards readers of today, we may agree with Brown: we do not know what the event signifies. Yet we can ask: how do readers choose to interpret it? The three narrative accounts of the rending of the veil in the New Testament touch upon some interesting issues, four of which will be examined here.

(a) The overarching questions is, of course, *how did the Evangelists interpret the death of Jesus?* If the writers of the Synoptic Gospels viewed the tearing of the veil as an act of God, the event should help us understand their interpretation of the suffering and death of Jesus.

(b) This immediately raises another problem. The event is mentioned in only three of the four New Testament Gospels—it does not occur in John—and there are important differences among the three Synoptic accounts (Greek *syn,* "same," and *opsis*, "view"). In the Lukan account, the rending of the veil takes place *before* the death of Jesus. In the Markan narrative, it occurs immediately *after* his death, and in the Matthean version it is followed by miracles: an earthquake and the resurrection of the dead in Jerusalem. If the most common interpretation were correct—that the rending of the veil meant Jesus' death opened the way to God—it would not have the support of the Lukan version, in which the veil is rent *before* the death of Jesus. Thus, we must ask ourselves, *what is the relation between the four Gospel accounts and their interpretations?*

7. For a list of interpretations, see Aus, *Samuel*, 156–57.

8. Hagner, *Matthew*, 2.849.

9. Brown, *Death of the Messiah*, 2.1102.

(c) Subsequently, this observation takes us to a more complex question: *what is the relation between "God's understanding" of the event and the interpretations of the Gospel authors?* In other words, since the four Evangelists do not concur, which version is to be preferred? That is, the readers' choice of *text* is also a choice of *theology.* How do we as readers cope with the fact that the same event is described so differently by three of the Evangelists—and not at all by the fourth?

(d) Yet more or less every interpretation emphasizes that the tearing of the veil was related to Jesus' death. Thus, we should also consider the possibilities and risks of *simultaneity as a hermeneutical key* when reading these texts. Why do we choose to interpret some events in terms of others, just because they happened at the same time, or on the same day?[10] It may seem unavoidable with the three Synoptic Gospels, but why is precisely this coincidence so well known? Is there only one way to explore a simultaneity? *Reichskristallnacht* was an attack on the Jews of Germany and Austria on the night between the 9th and 10th of November 1938.[11] Bishop Martin Sasse is said to have felt that burning the synagogues of Germany and Austria on the birthday of Martin Luther was an appropriate tribute to that great leader of the Reformation.[12] But what is important is not that events occur on the same day, but rather why we observe that they do, and what conclusions we draw from that simultaneity. It raises the question: *Why do so many interpreters choose to emphasize the simultaneity of Jesus' death with the rending of the veil?*

These four major questions will be left unanswered for now. But we will consider them in the following discussion. Now let us present three interpretations of the rending of the veil and relate them to three sentiments, *wrath, joyfulness,* and *grief.*

1. A Sign of God's Wrath?

The first interpretation sees the torn temple curtain as a consequence and expression of divine wrath in response to the betrayal and execution of

10. This motif is studied in Benktson's book *Samtidighetens mirakel.* Kierkegaard's simultaneity of factors is discussed (ibid., 396–97).

11. For more information on *Reichskristallnacht* (also called the November Pogrom), see Gilbert, *Kristallnacht.*

12. See Susannah Heschel, *Aryan Jesus,* 76. For Luther's view of Jewishness and Jewry, see Gritsch, *Martin Luther's Anti-Semitism.*

Jesus of Nazareth. Those who closely read the Gospels will soon notice their mention of religious and political groups that cooperated to get rid of Jesus, specifically representatives of temple leadership and the occupying Roman power. Yet this fact has not figured in any significant way in the eventual role of the texts in history. Rather, the Jewish people *as a whole* has been named, not as the people that Jesus knew as his own, but as his cynical executioners. This shift of emphasis can be detected in the canonical Gospels, but it is more palpable in the texts of the second century. For three reasons, Melito's Easter homily *Peri Pascha* (On Easter) is normally mentioned in this context, firstly, because it was written by an influential leader of the church. Melito (d. 180) was the bishop of Sardis, a city known in the Turkey of today as Sart Mustafa.[13] Secondly, it is a text that clearly accuses Jews *as a people* of the death of Jesus. Thirdly, the text is characterized by a *high Christology,* meaning that Jesus is more than human. In presentations of high Christology, emphasis is placed on the God in Christ. Therefore, not just anyone was executed on the cross; *God* was murdered there.[14]

> But you cast your vote against your Lord.
> For him whom the gentiles worshipped.
> And uncircumcised men admired
> And foreigners glorified,
> Over whom even
> Pilate washed his hands,
> You killed him at the great feast. . . .
> You killed your Lord in the middle of Jerusalem. . . .
> Listen, all you families of the nations, and see!
> An unprecedented (Greek *kainos*; i.e., "new," meaning "unparalleled") murder has occurred in the middle of Jerusalem.
> In the city of the law.
> In the city of the Hebrews.
> In the city of the prophets,
> In the city accounted just.
> And who has been murdered? Who is the murderer? . . .
> He who hung the earth is hanging;

13. Melito is sometimes spelled Meliton, which includes the last letter of his Greek name (as Plato is sometimes spelled Platon). Sardis was the capital of the ancient kingdom of Lydia. The synagogue, which was rediscovered in 1962, is 120 meters long and 18 meters wide. It had space for about a thousand worshippers. According to a manuscript written by Josephus, the Jewish congregation had been in Sardis "since the beginning" (Greek *ap' archēs*); see *Antiquitates Judaicae* 14.259–61.

14. See Werner, "Melito of Sardis."

> He who fixed the heavens has been fixed;
> He who fastened the universe has been fastened to a tree;
> The Sovereign has been insulted;
> The God has been murdered;
> The King of Israel has been put to death
> by an Israelite right hand.[15]
> O unprecedented (*kainou*) murder! Unprecedented (*kainēs*)
> crime![16]

As observed by Jeremy Cohen and others, only Jews are clearly singled out for this heinous crime and murder in this text. Non-Jews—described as "gentiles," "uncircumcised," and "strangers"—worship and honor him, but the Jewish people killed him during the grandest of all Jewish feasts. Thus, only one group stands accused of this heinous crime: the Jews—and of that group, every single member.

> Though the gospel stories of the Crucifixion allot important roles to Pilate and his Roman soldiers, Melito gives them no mention. He condemns Israel and Israel alone.[17]

Melito's Easter homily is an aggressive and condemning interpretation of the death of Jesus. God's wrath is upon the Jews for what they did. They did not see God in Christ and therefore lost the right to call themselves Israel: "But you did not turn out to be 'Israel'; you did not 'see God.'"[18] The background to this verdict is probably the popular—but without doubt etymologically incorrect—view that the Hebrew word *Yisrael* should be interpreted as *ish raah El* (the one who saw God).

Unfortunately, Melito's Easter homily is not an exception. Rather, the legal proceedings against Jesus are often presented in a way that it becomes a court case in which Jews stand accused: yesterday's Jews, today's Jews, all Jews of all times are accused of the death of Jesus. Bishop Melito's Easter homily raises many questions, of which only three can be considered here. What were his sources? What were the relations between Jews and

15. The Greek words *hypo dexias Israēlitidos* are literally "by an Israelite right hand." It could be that Melito wants to emphasize the force and power of Israel by explicitly writing *dexias*. Cf. Ps 73:23: "Nevertheless I am continually with you; you hold my right (Hebrew *yemini*) hand."

16. Melito, *On Pascha*, 92–97. For Greek text and English translation, see Melito of Sardis, *On Pascha and Fragments*.

17. Jeremy Cohen, *Christ Killers*, 59.

18. Melito, *On Pascha*, 82. Cf. Exod 32:30 and Philo, *Change of Names*, 81.

Christians in Sardis when he wrote his sermon? Was it actually a matter of living Jews or a question of rhetorical characters? Did he have flesh-and-blood people in mind—or not?

The Sources of Melito's Peri Pascha

Why does Melito direct his accusations only against the Jewish people, when it is so obvious in the New Testament Gospels that Roman soldiers actually carried out the execution? Othmar Perler has argued that the source of Melito's homily is not primarily the canonical Gospels but the apocryphal Gospel of Peter.[19] This text was rediscovered in 1886–87 in a tomb in Akhmim, Egypt, and there is good reason to assume, according to Perler, that Melito's Easter sermon is inspired by it. If Perler is correct, then this apocryphal gospel has played a tremendously important role in the Christian tradition. For Melito's homily *Peri Pascha,* in turn, has inspired the so-called *Improperia* (Reproaches) in the Good Friday liturgy, blaming the Jewish people for the death of Jesus.[20]

What was found in the tomb in Akhmim in the 1880s was only a fragment of the original Gospel of Peter. The fragment commences in the middle of the trial against Jesus and concludes with the disciples going back home after the death of Jesus. What has been preserved, though, is enough for us to see the differences between this apocryphal gospel and the New Testament Gospels. One of these differences is found in the very first sentence: "But of the Jews, none washed their hands, neither Herod nor any one of his judges."[21] Then the author goes on to tell the story of how *the Jews* (Greek *hoi Ioudaioi*) tortured Jesus, put a purple gown on him, and crucified him between two criminals. In other words, the Roman soldiers have totally vanished from the scene. In the Gospel of Peter, it is *the Jews* who

19. Perler, "L'Evangile de Pierre et Méliton de Sardis." In Sweden, two books had been published by 1893 on this text. See Lundborg, *Det s. k. Petrusevangeliet* and Hedqvist, *Petrus evangelium*.

20. Cf. Mic 6:2–3, "for the LORD has a controversy with his people, and he will contend with Israel. O my people, what have I done to you?" Patrick J. Morrisroe, *Catholic Encyclopedia, s.v.*: "The Improperia are the reproaches which in the liturgy of the Office of Good Friday the Saviour is made to utter against the Jews [*sic*], who, in requital for all the Divine favors and particularly for the delivery from the bondage of Egypt and safe conduct into the Promised Land, inflicted on Him the ignominies of the Passion and a cruel death."

21. Gos. Pet. 1. Compare this statement with Melito's homily *On Pascha,* 77 and 92.

carry out the execution! In his commentary, published in 1893, Vilhelm Hedqvist describes the *Tendenz* of the Gospel of Peter.

> In general, it seems the author's greatest desire was to relieve Pontius Pilate of all guilt and lay it completely upon the Jews.[22]

It is most likely that Perler is correct. We have good reason to believe that Bishop Melito's source is the apocryphal Gospel of Peter. Completely clear, in all events, is that the Gospel of Peter cannot be aligned historically with the descriptions in the New Testament Gospels.

In other words, we can regard the homily of Melito of Sardis, known as *Peri Pascha*, as an initial draft of the *Improperia* tradition, which was developed over time. Perler has shown us good reason to allege a connection between the Gospel of Peter and *Peri Pascha*. This would mean that the tradition of reproaching Jews in the Good Friday service is not based on the canonical Gospels but on an apocryphal gospel that was never included in the collection of canonical writings nor accepted by early Christianity for the New Testament.

Jews and Christians in Sardis

In the third century there was a heated discussion among Christians about when to celebrate Easter. Christians could not agree when the Christian Easter should be celebrated. Was it necessary to celebrate it on the *date* in the Jewish calendar that Jesus died (the 14th in the month of *nisan*), or should it take place on the *day* that he died (a Friday)? The Quartodecimans (as in, the number fourteen) argued that it was crucial for the celebration to be on the exact day of the month, not on the correct day of the week.[23] Melito was a Quartodeciman. His Good Friday celebration (which was not necessarily always on a Friday) always concurred with the Jewish Passover meal. Simultaneity, as we have already noted, can affect the interpretation of texts and events. On the same day that Jews in Sardis were celebrating the departure from Egypt, one of the most important feasts in their calendar, Melito and his fellow Christians were commemorating and mourning the death of Jesus. This simultaneity may be discerned in the following passage from Melito's Easter homily.

22. Hedqvist, *Petrus evangelium*, 22.

23. Cf. Lev 23:5: "On the fourteenth day of the month" (Latin *quarta decima die mensis*).

> And you were making merry, while he was starving:
> You had wine to drink and bread to eat, he had vinegar and gall;
> Your face was bright, his was downcast;
> You were triumphant, he was afflicted;
> You were making music, he was being judged;
> You were giving up the beat, he was being nailed up;
> You were dancing; he was being buried;
> You were reclining on a soft couch, he in grave and coffin.[24]

This is not primarily about the Jews crucifying Jesus; rather; it is a reference to Christian Good Friday taking place on the very same day the Jews in Sardis during Melito's time celebrated Passover. What is mentioned in the last stanza ("You were reclining on a soft couch, he in grave and coffin") is in all probability a reference to the practice of eating the Passover meal while sitting or leaning comfortably, as a remembrance and a celebration of no longer being slaves in Egypt. Jews today are reminded of this at Passover when singing the song *mah nishtanah ha-lailah ha-zeh mi-kol ha-leilot?* (Why is this night different from all other nights?) One of the questions posed by the youngest son is, "Why on this night are we all reclining?" The above interpretation can be called a sociohistorical interpretation, because it emphasizes that the text has been influenced by the actual situation in Sardis during the time of Bishop Melito in the third century.

Is this the principal rationale for the aggression in Melito's Easter homily? The fact that Jews were celebrating Passover in the very same city, perhaps in directly adjacent homes, might have seemed to call into question his triumphalist interpretation of Christianity, which replaced the old order with the new. Cohen explains,

> For when the Jews of Sardis relived the Exodus at their Passover seder on the very night that the Quartodeciman Melito conducted the Easter vigil in his church, they implicitly declared that Christianity's New Testament had not replaced the Old.[25]

In other words, Cohen argues that the historical simultaneity of celebrating Jewish Pesach simultaneously with Melito's Pascha was a theological challenge. "For Melito, that amounted to nothing less than killing Christ on the cross, again and again and again."[26]

24. Melito, *On Pascha*, 79–80.

25. Cohen, *Christ Killers*, 62.

26. Cohen, *Christ Killers*, 65. See also Boyarin, *Dying for God*, 13: "For these [Quartodeciman] Christians, Easter or Pascha was simply the correct way to observe the Pesah."

Real or Rhetorical Jews?

However, this raises another question: are the Jews that are described in the Gospel of Peter, and the Israelites described in *Peri Pascha,* real people or are they primarily rhetorical figures? Needless to say, real Jews have been the victims when Christians have read sacred texts during Holy Week, but the question posed now is a different one: does the text reflect the sociohistorical context in Sardis and other places? A number of scholars, (including Lynn Cohick, Paula Fredriksen, Judith Lieu, Adele Reinhartz, and Miriam Taylor) question whether early anti-Jewish texts primarily reflect actual conflicts between Jews and Christians.[27] Cohick writes that Melito's *Peri Pascha*

> centers on defining Christianity over against a hypothetical "Israel" that the unknown author has created largely for rhetorical purposes. . . . This homily's anti-Jewish rhetoric is not the place to find evidence for Jews or Judaism of its time.[28]

This highlights a problem with sociohistorical interpretation that constantly tends to seek a *historical* explanation for the *theological* outburst against Jews in Christian texts.[29] A parallel is that many New Testament scholars have argued that the reason for the Johannine Jews being described so negatively is that the Jews whom the Evangelist met were behaving badly toward the Johannine Christians.[30] Cohick argues that the maxim of these scholars appears to be "where there's smoke, there's fire."[31] In other words, the tone of the Christian texts must stem from a belief that Jews deserve reproach, even assault. To make use of a well-known biblical saying, in this situation it would appear that the one who was *not* free from sin threw the first stone.[32] Some people *act* provocatively, while others simply *react* legitimately in a tight spot.

27. See Fredriksen, "*Excaecati*," 322; Taylor, *Anti-Judaism*, 8; Lieu, *Image & Reality*, 199–240; Cohick, "PERI PASCHA"; and Reinhartz, "Fourth Gospel."

28. Cohick, "PERI PASCHA," 372.

29. This has been suggested by Fredriksen, "*Excaecati*," 322: "To place Christian anti-Jewish invective in such a context is to rationalize it, to give it some sort of reasoned and reasonable explanation."

30. See John 8:44: "You [Jews] are from your father the devil, and you choose to do your father's desires. He was a murderer from the beginning and does not stand in the truth, because there is no truth in him."

31. Cohick, "PERI PASCHA," 365.

32. Cf. John 8:7: "Let anyone among you who is without sin be the first to throw a stone at her."

Is it not better to say that the hints of conflict between Jews and Christians in the Gospel of John had heightened by the time it was written, rather than to completely lay the blame on one group?

It has been suggested that the accusatory tone in Melito's Easter homily is because of Jews behaving badly toward Christians in Sardis. Irrespective of how many Jews and Christians there actually were in Sardis at that time, and the relations between these two groups, we can detect here a disturbing tendency to describe theological outbursts in a way that not only *explains* but also *justifies* them. Some people tend to excuse the texts of their faith communities by blaming the behavior of the other group. To repeat, some people act, while other people simply react.

For numerous readers of the Bible, *imitatio Dei* is a virtue. If the temple veil was rent as an expression of divine wrath over "the Jews" killing Jesus, why should Christians be more forbearing than God, according to this vicious logic?[33] Thus, the main problem with this first interpretation is that it easily leads to antagonism and perhaps even aggression against the Jewish people. Of this interpretation we can say that "the tree is known by its fruit."[34] It is time to look at the second interpretation.

2. A Reason for Joyfulness

Karl Barth was one of the most influential Christian theologians of the twentieth century. In his *Church Dogmatics,* he argues that there is a vast difference between, on the one hand, God's revelation and, on the other hand, religion—that is, between Christianity (which, according to his atypical nomenclature, strictly speaking is not a religion) and all other religious phenomena. A consequence of this strict dichotomy is that religiosity is something negative: a religious belief or behavior is not, as we might assume, an expression of a person's *belief,* but rather of his or her *unbelief.* The revelation of God is the abolition of religion.[35]

We must revisit this dichotomy in our discussion of the torn veil, because the Second Temple is often described in a Barthian way in theological

33. Gurtner, *Torn Veil,* 7: "Other scholars have suggested that the rending of the veil is simply an act of vengeance on the part of God for the unjust execution of his son."

34. Matt 12:33.

35. Barth, *Church Dogmatics,* I.2.280–361. An introduction to his "Revelation of God" can be found in Plantinga, *Christianity and Pluralism,* 223–24. Barth is quoted ibid., 223–42.

literature. The torn veil is described as the end of the (incorrect) era of religiosity and religious thinking. It reveals something completely different, something that has nothing at all to do with the temple. According to this view, the Second Temple—the shrine that Jesus visited, according to the Evangelists, and in which his disciples "always praised God"—became the symbol of humanity's vain efforts to reach out to God.[36] This line of thought seeks to suggest that the temple is defective by definition. What we have in this approach is a dogmatically motivated inability to appreciate not only the Second Temple but also Second Temple Judaism.

The death of Jesus is seen as the end of the era of erroneous religiosity and the torn veil is a sign of this. Something new has taken its place. In his book *The Torn Veil,* Gurtner summarizes the history of this development with these words: "One of the few points of agreement among scholars who address the rending of the veil is that whatever else it means, it surely refers to the cessation of the veil's function."[37] The traditional view he describes is that "there is a new *accessibility* to God created through the removal of the separating function of the inner veil."[38] The theological message is that now there is a theological accessibility which was lacking before the veil was torn. Examples of this in the history of interpretation are legion. For example, in his *Lectures on the Gospel of Matthew*, published in 1868, William Kelly writes that before the veil was torn, it had been "the symbol that man could not draw near to God."[39] This second interpretation means, accordingly, that the temple was a theological obstacle. The veil was torn because the temple did not facilitate, but rather hindered, true worship.

There is sometimes an implicit ecclesiastical critique in this discourse of the torn veil. Numerous Christians believe that there is too much bureaucracy in their churches, that the liturgy is too complicated or old-fashioned, or that church leaders hinder people from reaching God. These Christians, therefore, believe and argue that something new is needed, but this Christian self-criticism is sometimes expressed as a critique of Second Temple

36. Luke 24:53. It is worth noting that Abraham Joshua Heschel argued the exact opposite, that it is God who constantly seeks out humans. See *God in Search of Man*, 136–44.

37. Gurtner, *Torn Veil*, 47.

38. Gurtner, *Torn Veil*, 188 (italics added).

39. Kelly, *Lectures on the Gospel of Matthew*, 398, quoted in Gurtner, *Torn Veil*, 15.

Judaism.[40] Still, there are several important objections to this influential and widespread interpretation.

The Anachronistic Fallacy

First and foremost, it should be pointed out that Jewish temple service was one of the few phenomena in Judaism that the surrounding cultures did *not* see as strange. Non-Jewish contemporaries saw Judaism as peculiar in many ways—*but that had nothing to do with the temple, nor with the offerings.*[41] On that point they agreed. It was more difficult to understand circumcision, food regulations, and the Sabbath, as pointed out by Paula Fredriksen:

> The thing most foreign to modern Western religiousness about ancient Judaism—the sacrifices and their attendant purity regulations—struck ancient observers as one of the few normal things Jews did.[42]

Anachronistic interpretations are widespread, not least on the Internet, which hosts a lot of simplistic interpretations of the torn veil. One example is the following text.

> The torn veil is the final verdict,
> Confirmed by the empty tomb three days later,
> The old ways are DEAD
> NO LONGER ARE WE SEPARATED FROM GOD
> Hallelujah!
> Rejoice!
> With the Torn Veil and the Empty Tomb GOD said it loud and clear:
> "No mortal, No Institution, No rules or laws, No human frailty
> Will come between ME and My Children"
> "You are free to seek Me EVERYWHERE!"
> Amen![43]

40. See Nirenberg, *Anti-Judaism*, e.g., 254: "After all, Jews and their synagogue had long been the whipping boys of preachers and exegetes" and 259: "The strategy of Judaizing Christian 'error' is as old as Christianity itself."

41. See Schäfer, *Judeophobia*.

42. Fredriksen, *Jesus of Nazareth*, 52.

43. www.youtube.com/watch?v=SU1mSKuwNNo (uppercased in original; accessed September 23, 2010).

The temple of Jerusalem is presented here as an institution that was blocking the path between human beings and God. A similar theological reasoning is expressed in the following text:

> The curtain separated a holy God from sinful man.
> *Man created the veil by turning against God.*
> But he could not tear it down.
> It was too high
> and too thick.
> It was said that even the strongest horses tied to each side . . .
> could not pull the veil apart.
> Only *God* could tear the veil. . . .
> The barrier between *God* & humanity was removed.
> The veil was torn.[44]

The veil is presented not only as a hindrance, but also as the very symbol of a people willfully turning away from God. Here, though, the author clashes with the Bible, because God ordered the people to build a tabernacle and gave quite exact instructions on how to build it. The specific instructions on how to build the tabernacle can be found in Exodus 26:31–33. In the thirty-first verse it is written, "You shall make a curtain of blue, purple, and crimson yarns, and of fine twisted linen; it shall be made with cherubim skillfully worked into it. . . . [A]nd the curtain shall separate for you the holy place from the most holy."[45] In other words, the supersessionist critique of the temple is so important in this line of thought that it induces its advocates to neglect what is quite obvious in the Bible: that *building the tabernacle was assigned by God and instructed by God.* Anyone trying to avoid an anachronistic approach soon discovers that, in the biblical narrative, the tabernacle and the temple are places of divine encounter, not symbols of the opposite. They make it possible for humans to *draw near* to God. They are not obstacles that *distance* people from God.[46]

44. Stevers, "The Veil."

45. Exod 26:31.

46. See Ps 84:1–2 and 4: "How lovely is your dwelling place, O LORD of hosts! My soul longs, indeed it faints for the courts of the LORD; my heart and my flesh sing for joy to the living God. . . . Happy are those who live in your house, ever singing your praise."

Redefining Key Concepts

Reinterpretations and semantic shifts provide opportunities to study a phenomenon closely. One example of this is when Gurtner wishes to describe the Matthean understanding of the temple. "This, however, is not a *rejection* of the temple. . . . Instead, it is an indication that the temple is *superfluous*: What it was intended to accomplish is *surpassed* by Jesus."[47] We have to ask ourselves, however, whether there is such a vast difference between these two statements. Gurtner describes the torn veil (Latin *velum scissum*) in the following manner.

> I can note here that the cessation of functions depicted by the *velum scissum* indicates, in some way, the cessation of the cultic necessity of distinctions between most holy and less holy, which therefore removes the need for such distinctions to be executed by a prohibition of physical and visual accessibility to God and removes the cherubim that graphically depicts this distinction.[48]

In the same book, Gurtner describes Matthean Christology: "For Matthew, Jesus is the true Israel and the people of God are defined by their relationship to Jesus."[49] This would mean that a people no longer consisted of individuals, together forming what Benedict Andersons calls "an imagined community"; instead, they are embodied in an individual.[50]

Jesus is described in a similar way by N. T. Wright as "a new David, who will rescue his people from their exile, that is, 'wave his people from their sins.'"[51] This immediately raises the question of why the word "exile" no longer means "deportation" but is spiritualized instead. The obvious answer is that, otherwise, the theological scheme simply does not work. The sad irony is that Christianity concurred not with the end of an exile of the Jewish people but with its beginning. As we all know, it was after the two revolts against the Romans (66–73 CE and 132–135 CE) that a new era of exile began for the Jewish people. It is always disquieting when words no longer have anything to do with their established meanings. These interpretations of the torn veil constitute no exception.

47. Gurtner, *Torn Veil*, 190 (italics added).

48. Gurtner, *Torn Veil*, 71.

49. Gurtner, *Torn Veil*, 198.

50. Benedict Anderson, *Imagined Communities*.

51. Wright, *New Testament and People of God*, 386.

The Problem of the Concept of "Revelation" in Religious Discourse

One of Ernst Käsemann's most famous assertions is that apocalypticism is the mother tongue of Christianity.[52] Christians have begun to speak other languages as well, but the fact is that a central idea in the theology of many Christians is the apocalyptic motif (from the Greek *apo*, "away from" or "back," and *kalypsis*, "veil")—the theological revelation. In this category we can place 1 Corinthians 2:9, in which verse Paul declares that he speaks, "as it is written, '*What no eye has seen, nor ear heard*, nor the human heart conceived.'"[53] This Christian proclamation per se is apocalyptic, that is, *revealing*. Is this the reason why many Christians understand the torn veil as a revelation—as an *euangelion*, a message of joy—although it took place on the very day that Jesus was humiliated, tortured, and executed? Is it possible that a theology that underscores the importance of revelation has a tendency of being so triumphalist as to be obtuse—and thereby failing to take suffering seriously, even on Good Friday?[54] We would not want the concept of revelation, which may at times be regarded as a piece of property belonging to the believer, to be used as a weapon against other people and peoples in order to defend and extol one's own denomination, perhaps even the individual theologian.[55] There is much to suggest that this second interpretation comprises such traits. It tends to be, in the words of H. Richard Niebuhr, "truths about God" instead of "divine self-disclosure."[56]

52. Käsemann, *New Testament Questions*, 102. Apocalypticism can be defined as the expectation that God's imminent intervention will destroy the ruling powers of evil and resurrect the righteous for final judgment. Cf. Acts 1:6: "Lord, is this the time when you will restore the kingdom to Israel?" Apocalypticism is a kind of eschatology (Greek *ta eschata*, "the final [things]" and *logos*, "word," "doctrine," or "doctrine of destiny").

53. 1 Cor 2:9. This is not quoted word for word but is probably a paraphrase of Isa 64:4. It is interesting to note that the message is slightly different in the parallel text in the Gospel of Thomas, which is directed toward the future (log. 17): "Jesus said, 'I shall give (Coptic *tinati*) you that no eye has seen . . .'" See Frid and Svartvik, *Thomasevangeliet*, 57 and 163–64.

54. For a short summary of what Niebuhr believes "revelation" (Latin *revelatio*; Greek *apokalypsis*) means and does not mean. See his *Meaning of Revelation*, e.g., xxiv, 20, 47, 80, 92, and 99. On p. 80 he describes revelation as "the moment in our history through which we know ourselves to be known from beginning to end, in which we are apprehended by the knower; it means the self-disclosing of that eternal knower." For additional viewpoints, see Svartvik, "Rendering," 268–70.

55. Niebuhr, *Meaning of Revelation*, 20 and 92.

56. Niebuhr, *Meaning of Revelation*, 95.

Gurtner's analysis is a thorough and well-written study of the Matthean version of the rending of the veil; however, his conclusion that the death of Jesus implies the end of the era of the temple is not unusual. He writes that it is an understanding he shares with a majority of New Testament scholars: "one of the few points of agreement among scholars who address the rending of the veil is that whatever else it means, it surely refers to the *cessation* of the veil's function."[57]

It must nevertheless be asked if this is the only possible conclusion. The temple fulfilled an important function for Jews in antiquity, and temple metaphors are still exceedingly important for Jews today. Can adherents to this interpretation genuinely seek to understand and appreciate the Jewish tradition? Or are the two alternatives mutually exclusive? Is it necessary to think of it as a crossroads whereby choosing one road eliminates the other?

The troubling question that remains is whether it is genuine *joyfulness* Christians are supposed to feel at the foot of the cross. If yes, what are the consequences for Christian views of torture and human suffering today? Are not the emotions we experience when encountering and pondering pain and agony in our world completely different from joy? This leads us to the third interpretation.

3. An Expression of Divine Sorrow?

Is there a third possibility? Can the tearing of the veil be a sign of or cause other feelings than the experience of divine wrath or human joy? To prepare for a third interpretation, we should reflect on what the torn veil might symbolize. In Judaism there is an ancient tradition of tearing one's clothing when death appears. The Hebrew term for this is *qeri'ah*. Nowadays this is done before or just after the funeral, or at the grave site, but in previous times it was at the time of death or upon hearing of the death that mourners tore their clothes.[58] This is described for example in 2 Samuel.

> While they were on the way, the report came to David that Absalom had killed all the king's sons, and not one of them was left. The king rose, tore his garments (Hebrew *wa-yiqra' begadaw*), and lay

57. Gurtner, *Torn Veil*, 47 (italics added).

58. For a brief introduction, see Klein, *Guide to Jewish*, 278–79, and Ozarowski, "*Keri'ah*: The Tearing of the Garment."

> on the ground; and all his servants who were standing by tore their garments (Hebrew *qeruʿei begadim*).[59]

For multiple reasons 2 Kings 2:12 is of special interest to us when pondering the New Testament passion narratives. First, it is about Elijah (who is mentioned in the passion narratives in the New Testament). Second, the mourner tears his clothes. Third, he tears them into two pieces. And fourth, a "father" is mentioned.

> Elisha kept watching [as Elijah ascended in a whirlwind into heaven] and crying out "Father, father! The chariots of Israel and its horsemen!" But when he could no longer see him, he grasped his own clothes and tore them in two pieces.[60]

God, too, shows divine grief by tearing garments. In the words of Roger David Aus, "It was natural for the rabbis to think that God in mourning rent His royal purple garment in heaven when His dwelling on earth, the Temple, was destroyed by the Babylonians."[61] Hence, the Jewish tradition of tearing one's clothes must be considered when interpreting the torn veil in the New Testament.

The point has been made several times in this book that the temple was a manifestation of divine presence. It was a meeting place between God and humans, not a hiding place for God. The temple—and its curtain—was not something that separated humans from God. To the contrary, the temple and its curtain were symbols of the *presence* of God, not a divine *absence*.[62]

Seeing the temple as the manifestation of divine presence, it is not difficult to imagine that the tearing of the veil can have been experienced as an expression of sorrow. God tore the divine robe when Jesus died.[63] Therefore, David Daube makes a convincing point.

59. 2 Sam 13:30–31.

60. 2 Kgs 2:12 (Hebrew *wa-yiqraʿem li-shnayim qeraʿim*; Greek [Septuagint]: *kai dierrēxen auta eis duo rhēgmata*). For additional viewpoints, see Daube, *New Testament*, 23.

61. Aus, *Samuel*, 151. Gurtner considers this assertion to be "highly speculative," see *Torn Veil*, 186.

62. Milgrom, *Numbers*, 20: "Since the inner Tabernacle curtains were anointed (Lev 8:10), they theoretically had the same sacred status as the sancta (Exod 30:29)."

63. Daube, *New Testament*, 25. Daube points out that "the word *pargodh*, which in the Targum stands for the curtain separating the holy of holies from the outer chamber, may also denote a tunic."

> When we consider the stress laid in the New Testament on the complete splitting of the curtain into two—or, according to some readings, two parts—from top to bottom, it is safe to find here an allusion to the rite practiced as a sign of deepest sorrow.[64]

An interesting connection is noted by Abraham Joshua Heschel in *Heavenly Torah.* He cites a medieval text that highlights the similarities between the two words *qeri'ah* (tearing, rupturing) and *raqia'* (stronghold, firmament) that is used in creation narrative. "And God said, 'Let there be a dome in the midst of the waters, and let it separate the waters from the waters.'"[65] This connection can be seen in Matthew. In the hour of heavenly grief, as God rends the divine garment in mourning (*qeri'ah*), the "dome" (*raqia'*) trembles. The latter is reflected in the reference to an earthquake.[66] In the presence of death, everything is torn in two.

According to this third interpretation, the rending of the veil may be understood as an expression of divine grief over what is happening. This has been suggested by several interpreters, including Claude G. Montefiore, David Daube, Roger David Aus, Rosann M. Catalano, and Paula Fredriksen.[67]

Yet another person who supports this thesis is, surprisingly, Melito of Sardis. In his *Peri Pascha* there is a passage that is relevant to this discussion. Melito's tone is reproachful of the Jewish people, yet it is nonetheless interesting to note the description of the one who grieves in the place of humans.

> For when the people did not tremble, the earth quaked;[68]
> When the people were not terrified, the heavens were terrified;

64. Daube, *New Testament*, 24. For a list of occasions of particularly great sorrow: *Mishnah Sanhedrin* 7.5, *Talmud Bavli Bava Qamma* 25b and *Mo'ed Qatan* 26a.

65. Gen 1:6. Heschel, *Heavenly Torah*, 124. See also the translator's note 46 on the same page.

66. Matt 27:51: "At that moment the curtain of the temple was torn in two, from top to bottom. The earth shook, and the rocks were split."

67. Daube, *New Testament*, 23–26; Fredriksen, *From Jesus to Christ*, 183; Aus, *Samuel*, 147–57; and, Catalano, "Matter of Perspective," 195. Most often, however, the rent veil is seen as an expression of divine grief that the temple will soon be destroyed. The first modern commentator to suggest the tearing of the veil was an expression of grief was most likely Claude G. Montefiore. See *Synoptic Gospels*, 2.388. For a bibliography of early Christian writing that interprets the rending of the veil as an expression of grief, see Gurtner, *Torn Veil*, 18 n.98.

68. It is possible we even find a definition of *raqia'* in Melito's text.

> *When the people did not tear their clothes, the angel tore his.*[69]
> When the people did not lament, the Lord thundered out of heaven and the Highest gave voice.[70]

In this antithetical presentation, one of God's angels fulfills what the people should have done. Melito contends that the veil is rent because God's angel rends his clothes in mourning when Jesus dies. In Melito's indisputably reproachful text we find these three small words in Greek: *perieschisato ho angelos* (angel tore [his garment]), proving that this third interpretation can be traced all the way back to the second century.

Words of Reconciliation

Paul writes in 2 Corinthians 5:19 that God has entrusted him with *ton logon tēs katallagēs* (the message of reconciliation).[71] This is often regarded as a reference to a Christian proclamation of reconciliation. But could we also see in this concise expression an exhortation to explain the biblical texts and message in a way that deepens understanding and allows them to promote reconciliation? If so, it would be apt when interpreting what happened at the time of the death of Jesus. It would prevent isolating the contents of the message from the reactions that are provoked among readers and listeners. Under the heading of being entrusted with the words of reconciliation, we will now study the consequences of the three key words: *wrath, joyfulness,* and *grief.*

In his book *Holy Week Preaching*, Krister Stendahl writes that the emphasis should be on the *consequences* of the events. "The mood is finality, not causality, as is the case so often in the Scriptures and in the teaching of Jesus."[72] Questions that emphasize *causality* focus on what led to the death of Jesus—what did they do then and there?—but those that emphasize *finality* investigate the consequences of his death—what does this mean for those who want to live as his disciples? In other words, he suggests that readers not ask so often "why?" as "what for?" Not so often "whence" as "whither?" In this chapter, three words have been in focus: wrath, joyfulness, and grief. Is it possible to describe the three interpretations in terms

69. Italics added (Greek *tou laou mē perieschismenou perieschisato ho angelos*).

70. Melito, *On Pascha*, 98.

71. 2 Cor 5:19.

72. Stendahl, *Holy Week Preaching*, 23.

of "whither"? What are the consequences? Where to they take us? "When Christians come to the foot of the cross of Jesus," says Catalano, "they need a piety that honors God and all those whom God loves."[73]

(a) The first interpretation, which centers on divine wrath, triggers a loaded question: Why is God so angry that the veil is torn, all the way from the top to the bottom? What feelings arise within the reader? We all know that Holy Week has been anything but holy for Jews. Indeed, for two thousand years it has been a *Via Dolorosa* (Way of Suffering). The main cause of this suffering is that Christians have been convinced that Jews as a people are collectively responsible for the death of Jesus. Writers who argue that the wrath of God at what happened during Holy Week is demonstrated by the torn veil are likely to evoke a similar anger in their readers. The history of the outcome of this first interpretation reveals how problematic and dangerous it is.

(b) The second interpretation, focusing on human joyfulness, presents the temple as an obstacle to people's relation with God. The temple that stood at the time of Jesus is portrayed as the principal symbol of people's disbelief and lack of faith. This is a highly anachronistic interpretation, as observed earlier. In antiquity, and especially in biblical times, temples were places for holy encounters. Temples were like the horizon, that is, the place where heaven and earth met. This interpretation is also problematic in that it tends not to take suffering and grief seriously. Is there a risk that a theology that overemphasizes revelation might make us indifferent to suffering and death? Is there a risk that it leads to an insensitive elation, a merciless and triumphalist superiority?

(c) The third interpretation suggests that the torn veil could be understood as an expression of divine grief over the death of Jesus. Readers would react very differently to this than to the interpretation of divine wrath. If divine grief is at the center, readers will ask themselves a very different sort of question: Why does God grieve so much? What occasions divine sorrow at this moment in the narrative? A Jewish text written a few generations following the death of Jesus reads, "When a single human being dies, it is as though a whole world dies."[74] The reader who believes that *imitatio Dei* is the appropriate behavior is thereby introduced to another

73. Catalano, "Matter of Perspective," 198.

74. *Mishnah Sanhedrin* 4.5. The text continues, "and whoever saves a single human being, Scripture credits this person as though a whole world has been saved." This section from Mishnah is often cited in Jewish contexts, such as on the memorial for Raoul Wallenberg at Yad Vashem in Jerusalem.

way of thinking—that of mourning the death of the next human being as if an entire world has died, letting this grief be transformed into caring for other people, and remembering that every human being is a microcosm, a small world.[75]

In one of Abraham Joshua Heschel's poems we find a similar connection between a God who expresses divine *sorrow* by a rending of clothes and the exhortation to *care* for other people. These words may serve as a reminder that *theology* should never be isolated from *ethics*—and of the importance of feeling the next person's suffering as one's own. Translated from the original Yiddish:

> Like sparked logs lusting, thirsting for flames
> my eyes cry to You, God.
> Who rends His clothes in mourning for the world—
> Let us see how Your face is mirrored
> in the pupils of our eyes.
>
> And I have sworn:
> to let the pupils of my eyes to be mirror to each sunset,
> my heart never sealed
> my eyes never locked![76]

In this and previous chapters, two drastic motifs have been examined. One is the statement in Ephesians that a dividing wall has fallen. The other is the narrative in the Synoptic Gospels of the curtain in the temple tearing at the time of Jesus' death. We have seen that there is good reason to understand the fallen dividing wall in the light of a section from 2 Baruch, written approximately the same time, which describes that when a human being is enlightened, it is as if a wall of ignorance has crumbled. Given that the author of Ephesians writes that those who were once far off are brought near through the life and teachings of Jesus, it is logical to assume that the fallen wall refers to gentiles now being brought near the God of Israel. In this chapter we have seen that the scripture about the veil in the temple tearing

75. Cf. Catalano, "Matter of Perspective," 196: "The question the text occasions is not 'Why is God angry?' but 'What is God mourning?' What occasions divine sorrow at this moment in the narrative?" For the view of the human being as a microcosm and the church as *makro-anthrōpos* (macrobeing), see Lossky, *Mystical Theology*, 114 and 178.

76. Heschel, "Untitled" (Yiddish *On a nomen*), *The Ineffable Name of God*, 193. The replacement of second (Yiddish *tsu dir*; English *to You*) and third person (Yiddish *zikh*; English *His*) may reflect the way Jewish prayers transition from second to third person. For example, "Blessed be *you* . . . who consecrate us by *his* laws."

at the time of Jesus' death can be interpreted as an expression of divine empathy. In other words, neither the fallen wall nor the torn veil are about true contact with God being possible only upon the death of Jesus.

Gospel, Causality, and Finality

We use the word "gospel' in different ways. In everyday speech, it refers primarily to four of the New Testament books, namely the narratives of Jesus' life and death that are attributed to Evangelists Matthew, Mark, Luke, and John. Evangelist comes from the Greek *euangelion,* which means "good news." For what reason are the Gospels written by the evangelists' considered to be good news?

We return now to the concepts of causality and finality. Causality here refers to that which led to the events of Good Friday. Finality refers instead to the consequences of Good Friday. What is the causality and what is the finality of the crucifixion? There is a risk that an isolationistic Good Friday theology confuses history and theology. How critical is it actually for theology to determine why Jesus died? The ongoing discussion of this among New Testament scholars is called *crucifiability.*[77] This word refers to the assumption that there must exist—and that it must be possible to determine using historical research methods—sufficient explanation for the crucifixion of Jesus. We tend to forget that Pontius Pilate was a brutal despot who was notorious for habitually ordering executions without proper trials. Joseph B. Tyson makes the following conclusion.

> Jesus was put to death under the authority of the Roman governor, Pontius Pilate, for an alleged violation of Roman law. . . . Jesus' death was not brought about by *Jewish opposition* but rather by *Roman political oppression.*[78]

The Roman military government made a politically motivated—and more or less well-grounded—decision: before Jewish Passover it made sense

77. A more correct expression is *criterion of crucifiability.* The unexpressed premise is that there must be logical reasons for people being imprisoned and killed during an occupation. But can we really assume that the Romans always had an explicit reason for wanting to get rid of everyone they had executed? See Gaston, "The Uniqueness of Jesus as a Methodological Problem," 276: "History knows too many examples of meaningless deaths, of the execution of the innocent, of judicial mistakes, for this not to be an equally plausible explanation."

78. Tyson, "Death of Jesus," 44 and 45 (italics added).

for security reasons to get rid of yet another Jewish agitator. Already, for historical reasons, it is getting complicated to ask, why was Jesus killed?

In addition, if we ask *only* the historical question, the consequence becomes that we emphasize the historical causality of the cross at the expense of that which is very much more important, namely its theological finality. Historians can—and should—of course do their best to try to answer the question of why Jesus was executed by the Romans on a cross, but neither the question nor the proposed explanations are necessarily relevant to Christian theology. Focusing *solely* on the causality of the crucifixion is insufficient theologically and thus unsatisfactory when it is so obvious that the finality of the crucifixion is the subject of the early Christian writings.

There is good reason to argue that the causality of the crucifixion has more to do with the Gospels as a literary genre than as the bearers of good news. In other words, it is the Evangelists' narrative, storytelling form and format that causes the authors to emphasize causality. What makes a story a story, as Edward Morgan Forster writes in his book *Aspects of the Novel*, is that there is a *plot,* meaning that the author develops, and the reader discovers a causal connection between what we typically call "cause" and "effect." Forster's famous example is that the sentence, "The king died and then the queen died," has no plot. However, there is a plot in the sentence, "The king died and then the queen died *of grief*." In other words, in narrative presentations there is causality, a chain of events.[79] Does this apply as well to the New Testament evangelists? The Gospels contain a description of the conflict between Jesus and the Roman and Jewish leadership because the evangelistic genre demands it. Yet a mere glance at the Pauline epistles proves it is not the *only* way to talk about the life, death, and resurrection of Jesus. In short, the narrative genre causes the reader to expect a plot—and in the Gospels, the plot is also one of plotting intrigue.

Gospel Beginning and Continuation

The Gospel of Mark, which is the oldest narrative of the life and death of Jesus, starts with the words, "The beginning of the good news of Jesus Christ (Greek *archē tou euangeliou Iēsou Christou*)." The question is where the beginning actually ends. Does it end in the writing down of that sentence? Or the first paragraph? Should we perhaps assume that the entire

79. Forster, *Aspects of the Novel*, 87: "The time-sequence is preserved, but the sense of causality overshadows it."

first chapter is the beginning of the gospel? Is not the most convincing and thought-provoking interpretation that the entire Gospel of Mark is "the beginning of the gospel"? When this text was written, the Christians who read it already knew how it was going to end. They knew it led to Paul's mission among the gentiles. Those who heard the Gospel of Mark in the Christian congregations were convinced that they were no longer, in the words of Ephesians, "aliens from the commonwealth of Israel, and strangers to the covenants of promise, having no hope and without God in the world." Now they "who once were far off" had been "brought near."[80] Paul's letters had been circulating for several decades in the Pauline congregations, which already existed when Mark was written. Now these Christians wanted to know how it all began. This is likely exactly why Mark was written, and why it begins with the words, "The beginning." The last verses of the sixteenth chapter describe how the women coming to the grave find it empty. They had expected a presence but are terrified by an absence. "So they went out and fled from the tomb, for terror and amazement had seized them; and they said nothing to anyone, for they were afraid."[81] Though unexpressed, there is an understanding between the author of this gospel and the listeners and readers that this is still not the end. Eventually the women must have overcome their fear and begun to tell what they had seen and heard. This is why the *entire* gospel written by the Evangelist, Mark, is the beginning of the good news. This absence of presence—and a presence that seems to overcome absence—is fundamental to Christian self-conception. This is what we will examine in the next chapter.

80. Eph 2:12–13.

81. Mark 16:8. In the oldest handwritten manuscripts, the Gospel of Mark ends with the eighth verse.

8

"This Is . . . for You"

The purpose of this book is to study reconciliation and transformation. The time has now come to look at the consequences of these two concepts for the individual human being. Now, having investigated the offering rituals of the Hebrew Bible, the cross theologies of the New Testament, and Christian theories of reconciliation in the six previous chapters, the question is, what is the meaning of the words "This is my body that is for you"? To suggest answers to this question is the main task of this chapter. But first, a short summary of what has been established thus far about the Hebrew Bible and the New Testament scriptures.

Offering to Draw Near or Withdraw?

We must do justice to an often-misunderstood topic, namely the descriptions of offering in the Hebrew Bible. The Hebrew name for offering is *qorban* and has to do with "drawing close" (*le-hitqarev*). Sacrificial theologies and writings can be difficult for us to understand because sacrifice, especially of animals, is not the way of our times to approach God. And neither Jews nor Christians have offered animals to approach God since the fall of the temple in 70 CE. The risk of taking an anachronistic approach is therefore great, and much more so for Christians than Jews, because Jews by definition have a more loyal attitude toward the first five books of the Bible. The first five books make up the Torah, the core of Jewish belief and tradition. But Christians experience them differently. Christians tend to read the Old Testament texts when they seem relevant or as an extra resource. They include the unforgettable accounts in Genesis of the patriarchs and matriarchs. They include the books of the prophets, and many of the psalms. But it is rare that the instructions on offering are considered relevant. Many people who decide to read the entire Bible stop when they get to the instructions on offering in Leviticus. The irony is that these texts make some Christians feel *excluded*, when, strictly speaking, their intent is the complete opposite, that is, to *include*.

How should we then approach the fundamental concepts in the writings on offering? Moshe Halbertal's distinction between *offering as a gift to someone* and *offering as a means to achieve something* has proved enlightening. The offerings in the Hebrew Bible expressed an already-existing relationship between God and humanity. Different types of offerings are described: burnt offerings, food offerings, offerings of well-being, sin offerings, and guilt offerings. In short, offering was a way to manifest various aspects of the relationship between God and human beings. Not all offering was sin offering, as not all Christian prayer is confession of sin.[1]

Furthermore, we saw that the exception for the poorest of poor people demonstrated that blood was not an absolute condition for reconciliation and forgiveness. The sin offering was a manifestation of human confession of fault and the desire to repent (Hebrew *teshuvah*) on the one hand, and of God's mercy on the other. T. S. Eliot's words come to mind.

> There is only the fight to recover what has been lost
> And found and lost again and again: and now, under conditions
> That seem unpropitious. But perhaps neither gain nor loss.
> *For us, there is only the trying. The rest is not our business.*[2]

Altogether, the offering rituals in the Hebrew Bible and in the rabbinical discussions of them reveal a trust in God, who forgives and endows the rituals with meaning and purpose. An example of this is how the rabbinical literature describes the fundamental difference between the animal offerings in the temples of previous generations on the one hand, and on the other, human beings. In order for animals to be acceptable for offering, they had to be completely whole and faultless, but for human beings it is just the opposite. That it is *precisely* the broken human heart that is allowed to converse with God is emphasized in the Bible, and it is *particularly* the broken human being that must not be turned away.[3] In

1. For a brief discussion of the three words *thanks, help, and forgiveness,* see Svartvik, *Förundran*, 124–26.

2. Eliot, "East Coker, V," *Four Quartets*, 22 (italics added).

3. *Pesiqta de-Rav Kahana, Shuvah* 5 (= 24.5) and *Talmud Bavli Sanhedrin* 43b. See also Halbertal, *On Sacrifice*, 42–43.

the psalmist's words: "The sacrifice acceptable to God is a broken spirit; a broken and contrite heart, O God, you will not despise."[4]

The Cross: Trembling, Troubling, and Transformed Telling

In discussing New Testament content and narrative history, there is one event that is rooted undoubtedly at the core, namely the crucifixion of Jesus. Sometimes, if not often, the crucifixion has been read, interpreted, and applied in a deeply troubling way. How can Christians face this unavoidable fact? In the book *Redeeming Our Sacred Story,* Mary C. Boys suggests a three-part approach that can help people to read, interpret, and apply the accounts of the suffering and death of Jesus.

(a) First and most importantly, we must recognize that this event and the recounting of it are unavoidably central to Christian self-conception. These accounts describe the experience of Jesus as a human being. He was betrayed by those closest to him, he feared death, he seems to have exhibited uncertainty as to God's will, and he withstood horrific pain and a heinous method of execution. These are events and accounts that make Christians "tremble, tremble, tremble," in the words of the spiritual, "Were you there when they crucified my Lord?" Preaching the death and resurrection of Jesus make up the core of Christian liturgy, spirituality, profession of creed, and faith. For centuries, it has generated music, art, and writing. For an innumerable number of Christians throughout history and in our own times, the cross is the symbol of persevering resistance to poverty, degradation, and oppression. The symbol of the cross has been carved into the walls of prison cells all over the world by people in situations horrifyingly reminiscent of Jesus' last hours on earth, people who are imprisoned, mocked, demeaned, and tortured before being killed. The cross is a symbol that fills Christians with *dread.* Mary Boys uses the word "trembling" to summarize this insight. The cross is an expression of human faith, not just in something that provides the strength to live, but also endurance and faith in the face of death. It is an almost indescribably strong symbol of the

4. Ps 51:17. That a broken heart should not be *contrasted* with a sacrificial offering is clear in the following lines: "Then you will delight in right sacrifices, in burnt offerings and whole burnt offerings; then bulls will be offered on your altar."

presence of God in the most completely godforsaken place, by all worldly measures: a place of execution.[5]

(b) Second, the cross is a symbol with a *troubling* history. At one time, the cross was a symbol of the Romans' degrading method of executing the enemies of the empire, and it has remained a symbol of violence. Christians have tried to domesticate the cross, but it has continued to be an unruly symbol, one that has been used to excuse oppression, sanction violence, and romanticize suffering. Not least, the cross has been used against Jesus' own people in such a way that all Jews in all times have come to be accused of the death of Jesus.[6] It is a holy duty of all Christians to know that the cross has been used in this deeply problematic way. It is intellectually dishonorable to make the symbol of the cross one's own without considering the shadow the cross has cast—and still casts—over other groups.[7]

(c) The third point Boys makes is about *transformed tellings*. The cross is a symbol that is not only respected and scrutinized but also reconstructed. It is a symbol that not only induces dread and is troubling but can and should induce a semantic shift.[8] Boys names some of the tools we have at our disposal to reform cross theologies: we now have better knowledge of the historical situation in the time of Jesus; we know of the oppressive structures of the Roman empire; we know more about religious identity and the various groupings of the first centuries following the birth of Jesus; and we have developed methods to interpret and apply the accounts of the New Testament.[9]

The question now is in which way cross theologies can change and renew our thinking. In the New Testament, the cross is described as a stumbling block (Greek *skandalon*). In which way is it a stumbling block? In this chapter, three motifs will be presented, three *stumbling blocks* that could be *cornerstones* in a construction that does not sanction violence, does not romanticize suffering, and does not disarm its victims.

5. Boys, *Redeeming*, 9–44 ("Trembling Telling").

6. Svartvik, *Förundran*, 65–66.

7. Boys, *Redeeming*, 47–156 ("Troubling Telling").

8. Cone discussed this in *Cross*, 30–64 and 172–73 n.13. Niebuhr's view of the transvaluation of values in, e.g., *Nature and Destiny*. Cone is critical of Niebuhr's lack of interest and engagement in the situation of black Americans.

9. Boys, *Redeeming*, 159–256 ("Transformed Telling").

From Storm to Calm

We will take a look at three meetings with God in the Bible, then look into African American experiences of God, and finally consider the role of Holy Communion in this context.

Historically, Christian interpretations of the events of Good Friday have been primarily about appeasing the wrath of God and shifting a storm of wrath into a calm of reconciliation. But we have also seen that this is not the only interpretation. There are other motifs in the Bible and in the history of the church. Let us for a moment leave the stormy seas for calmer water to see what we can find there. What we find in the Bible is striking: meetings with God do not always happen *where*, *when*, and *how* humans expect to meet God. We can learn this from the stories of Jacob, Elijah, and Job.

Jacob's Life-Changing Meeting in the Dark

In Genesis 32, Jacob wrestles with a person all night until daybreak. Throughout the ages, readers of the Bible have wondered who wrestled with Jacob. Who could it be? (a) A first interpretation is that it is *his twin brother, Esau.* The twins are fighting already in the womb. "If it is to be this way, why do I live?" asks their mother, Rebekah.[10] When they grow up, Esau becomes the favorite of his father, Isaac—and Jacob the delight of his mother, Rebekah. The enmity between the brothers is the dominating story of the following chapters. Finally, Jacob prays. "Deliver me, please, from the hand of my brother, from the hand of Esau, for I am afraid of him; he may come and kill us all, the mothers with the children."[11] In the Swedish Bible 2000, the section is titled Jacob Wrestles with an Unknown (Swedish *Jakob brottas med en okänd*)—but this heading, of course, is not included in the original Hebrew. In the actual text is something that might point in the opposite direction. "But he said, 'Why is it that you ask my name?'"[12] It is as if he were saying, have we fought so much for so long that you no longer recognize me, your own brother? Until the thirty-second chapter, Jacob has been behaving as if he had forgotten his family and his

10. Gen 25:22. The Hebrew is difficult to interpret: *im-ken lamah zeh anokhi* (if so, why [am?] I so). For rabbinical discussions, see Zlotowitz and Scherman, *Bereishis*, 1.1052–3.

11. Gen 32:11.

12. Gen 32:30.

brother Esau. It is striking how differently the two mortal enemies meet and greet each other in the next chapter. Jacob goes ahead, bowing himself to the ground seven times, until he comes near his brother. But Esau runs to meet him and embraces him. He falls on his neck and kisses him, and they weep. Before the meeting in the night, Jacob prays to be delivered from his brother Esau, because he fears the brother will come and kill him. But after the meeting in the night, the brothers meet and are reconciled—and between these two accounts is the nightlong wrestling match. Could it be that he meets Esau during the night?

(b) Another possibility is that *he is ultimately fighting his own self.* He asks himself how he has behaved. What must he do to make things different? What wrongs must he put behind him? What, on the other hand, is so important that it must not be forgotten? What is most important? The verse of Jacob limping is about the battered brokenness in our lives. The Hebrew expression *tiqqun 'olam* (healing the world) has become very popular, not least among those who are engaged against injustices in our world, but there is another expression that is also important, namely *tiqqun 'atsmi* (healing oneself).[13] When Jacob is struck on the hip socket, he limps, perhaps for the rest of his life, yet he is as if reconciled and transformed. Though wounded he projects—in a different dimension—that he is healed after his night at the ford of the Jabbok.

(c) The most common interpretation is nonetheless that Jacob wrestled with an angel of God, that this is a text about *a human being's struggle with God.* "So Jacob called the place Peniel (God's face), saying, 'For I have seen God face to face (Hebrew *panim el-panim*), and yet my life is preserved.'"[14] Regardless of how we feel about the two previous interpretations—that the account is of a relation to one's fellow human or oneself—it is also an account of a meeting with God. It is worth noting that only after seeing God face to face and leaving Peniel does Jacob see the sun rise. The night seems to feel darkest and coldest just before dawn. Jacob's meeting with God takes place in the night, the deepest darkness. In the chapter on the rending of the veil in the temple, we noted a popular interpretation of the name Israel from *ish raah El* (the one who saw God). Though etymologically unlikely, it is worth observing. Jacob saw God—in the darkness. In Peter Shaffer's play *Equus,* the doctor says to a patient, "We need a story to see in the dark."[15]

13. For more information, see Dorff, *Way into* Tikkun Olam.

14. Gen 32:30.

15. Quoted in Robert M. Franklin, "African American Pilgrimage," 161.

The account of Jacob at the ford of the Jabbok is one of those stories. In the darkness, Jacob sees what "no eye has seen."[16]

It is possible to join all three interpretations in a fourth possibility, that is, that Jacob, in a showdown with *himself* that night could see *God* in *another person's* face. The wonder of it is that he is able to see God in his fellow human, rendering him *ish raah El.*[17] Is Jacob the one who meets both God and humanity at the same time? In the New Revised Standard Version, the Hebrew word *wa-* is translated "and yet." This would emphasize the idea of a fundamental dynamic in the account, "For I have seen God face to face, *and yet* my life is preserved." But it is just as possible to translate *wa-* with "and." In that moment, when Jacob is wrestling with himself in such a way that he sees God in another human being's face, his life is saved. When the divine and the human are united, he sees—in the darkest night—what no eye has seen.

Elijah and the Voice of a Quiet Silence

Another figure in the Hebrew Bible is the prophet, Elijah. When he finds himself in a difficult situation in 1 Kings, Elijah loses the will to live and wishes for death. He cries out. "It is enough; now, O Lord, take away my life, for I am no better than my ancestors."[18] Then follows what may be the most paradoxical description of a meeting with God in the Bible.

> He said, "Go out and stand on the mountain before the Lord, for the Lord is about to pass by." Now there was a great wind, so strong that it was splitting mountains and breaking rocks in pieces before the Lord, but the Lord was not in the wind; and after the wind an earthquake, but the Lord was not in the earthquake; and after the earthquake a fire, but the Lord was not in the fire; and after the fire a sound of sheer silence.[19]

16. Isa 64:4. Cf. 1 Cor 2:9. Cf. Lindberg, "Några drag i den ortodoxa kyrkans liv," 16: "Jacob's words at the ford of the Jabbok, 'I will not let you go, unless you bless me,' are a constant in Christian consciousness."

17. No one has emphasized the importance of seeing the "face" of the next human being as has the Jewish philosopher Emmanuel Levinas. In his emphasis on *visage* (French for "face") is the Hebrew *panim* with all of its associations (*li-phnei*, "in the presence of," "before"; *penim*, "inside of," etc.). See Eskenazi, "Introduction—Facing the Text as Other."

18. 1 Kgs 19:4.

19. 1 Kgs 19:11–12.

So often—both in scripture and in interpretations of scripture—astonishing marvels and sensational wonders are interpreted as acts of God.[20] Yet in this account there is something completely different. It is not exceptional because it is supernatural or unnatural but because it is completely unexpected—and paradoxical. God was in neither the great wind, nor the earthquake, nor the fire. The Hebrew behind the "sound of sheer silence" is *qol demamah daqqah,* which literally means "the voice of a quiet silence." Similar expressions that capture this paradoxical idea might be "a calm wind," "a dark light," or perhaps "a victorious defeat." When Elijah experiences the voice of this quiet silence, it is as if he has heard that which "no ear has perceived."[21]

In Jewish tradition, Elijah has been criticized. Especially compared to Moses, Elijah has been criticized for neither thinking nor speaking well of his people, and for failing to interpret everything in the best possible light.[22] When Moses meets God on Mount Sinai, he prays profoundly for his people. But Elijah categorically accuses all Israelites of having abandoned their covenant with God.[23] When a Jewish infant boy is circumcised on his eighth day of life, a chair is placed beside the person who is *sanddaq*, the one who either holds the boy or who hands over the boy to the *mohel*, the person who is to carry out the circumcision.[24] This chair is actually called *kisse shel Eliyahu* (Elijah's chair).[25] By one interpretation, this is because of the categorical way in which Elijah accused all his people of abandoning the covenant. That is why he is forced to witness every circumcision, which is a sign of the covenant between God and Israel. On Mount Horeb, Elijah

20. See the event described in the previous chapter (1 Kgs 18:30–38).

21. Isa 64:4. Cf. 1 Cor 2:9. Gillman compares the divine revelations in Exod 19 and 1 Kgs 19. He shares, as well, the interpretation that is attributed to the Hasidic rabbi Mendel av Rimanov. The rabbi held that the only thing revealed on Mount Sinai was the first commandment's—and the alphabet's—first letter, *alef.* This letter is not pronounced in postbiblical Hebrew. The letter alef is "the voice of a quiet silence." See *Believing*, 55–57. See also Jakubowski, *Ljudet av alef*, 12.

22. Cf. Martin Luther's discussion of the eighth commandment in *Martin Luther's Basic Theological Writings*, 321.

23. Cf. Exod 32:30–32 and 1 Kgs 19:10 and 14. Sinai and Horeb are different names of the same mountain where Moses received the commandments. See Exod 19–20 and Deut 5.

24. The word *sandaq* may stem from the Greek *syndikos* (commissioner or ombudsman; cf. Latin *syndicus*) or from *synteknon* (*syn* [with] and *teknon* [child]). Hebrew words that start with the letter *samekh* are often borrowed from other languages.

25. See *Pirqe de-Rabbi Eliezer* 29.

meets God when he hears what no ear has perceived. At every circumcision, he cannot avoid seeing what all others see, namely that God's covenant with the Jewish people is still in effect.[26]

Job and the Importance of Being Honest When Meeting God

Now let us turn to the main character in the Book of Job. In his comments, Johannes Lindblom called this book "a classic in suffering. Never has the subject been treated so completely or artfully."[27] The Book of Job, which gives voice to despair, is impregnated with unforgettable expressions. One of these is in the ninth chapter, in which a despondent Job cries out, "The earth is given into the hand of the wicked" (Hebrew *erets nittnah ve-yad rasha'*).[28] In other words, Job cries out from his bottomless disappointment over what has happened, by calling God *rasha'*. Job's complaints were too much for the translators of the Bible into Swedish in 1917. They chose to translate the noun that was in the singular to the plural (despite there being no writings that supported such a translation). "The earth is given into the hands of the wicked [i.e., people]." The reader gets the impression that Job is making some kind of social critique instead of what he is most likely doing: blaming *God* for what is going on in the world and for his misfortune.

At the close of the book, Job's colleagues are reprimanded, "for you have not spoken of me what is right, as my servant Job has."[29] This is truly worth noting! In all his pain and anger, in all his despair and anguish, Job has been speaking the truth—and for this he is noticed and appreciated. Although Job's friends have been saying what is normally said when we discuss suffering—namely, that there are reasons why we have to suffer and it is wrong to be expressing the feelings Job does—still, it is Job who gets the praise.

26. Cf. "Guds vägar," 122: "God's covenant with the Jewish people is still valid."

27. Lindblom, *Boken om Job*, 5.

28. Job 9:24. Cf. Whybray, *Job*, 67: "In the final phrase of v. 24 he holds God responsible for all the wickedness that is perpetrated: if he is the real ruler of the world, he alone must be responsible for everything that happens in it."

29. Job 42:7 and 8. The Hebrew is *lo dibbartem elay nekhonah ke-'avdi Iyyov*. For its interpretation, see Wolfers, *Deep Things*, 462: "This unexpected endorsement of Job's words about God will draw debate as long as memory of the book remains with mankind. It is open to every interpreter to state his own opinion as to what it was that Job said which drew this remark from the Lord." He describes the comments of the friends as "sentimental rubbish, at odds with all experience of life."

Edward L. Greenstein argues that the fundamental idea in this entire book of the Bible is that Job is the one who is telling the truth.[30]

There is more to wonder at in this verse. It may be that the Hebrew should not be translated into speaking the truth "*about* me" (which in Hebrew is usually *'alay*) but instead should be "*to* me" (*elay*). Then the meaning of the verse is even more astonishing. "For you have not spoken *to* me what is right, as my servant Job has."[31] Should we interpret this text such that Job has been honest and sincere, not only when he is speaking *about* God, but also when he is speaking *to* God? Is the text saying that Job has not been hypocritical, as the friends have? Is it ultimately this critique that is directed toward Job's friends? The criterion in the Book of Job is to be truthful about God (to speak correctly *about* God) and perhaps the scripture emphasizes how important it is to be truthful in meetings with God (to speak honestly and sincerely *with* God).[32]

Speaking the Truth about and with God

Can it be that the Book of Job emphasizes the importance of truthfully turning to God? The same idea is expressed in the Psalms.

> The LORD is *near* to all who call on him, to all who call on him *in truth*.[33]

What does it mean to call on God in truth (Hebrew *be-emet*)? Raphael Jospe has compared translations and noted that there are two main interpretations. In one of them it is only the person who *owns the truth* who has the possibility of being heard in prayer. But in the other, it is the

30. Greenstein, "Truth or Theodicy?" 258: "Job is the hero of the book because he speaks the truth no matter what the risk and the cost." But then, says Lindblom, "Some of the original account must be missing, because in the main dialogue, the friends actually defend God, while Job often lashes out in profane rebellion against God." See Lindblom, *Boken om Job*, 50. A possibility is that the "truth" (Hebrew *nekhonah*) is actually Job speaking in 42:5–6. See Whybray, *Job*, 193.

31. Cf. how the same preposition is used in Job 5:26, 15:22, and 29:19. For this interpretation, see Pelc, "'Talk to Me': Wisdom from the Book of Job 42," 50: "This is a revolutionary revelation, as Job is praised for the *direction* of his speech (toward God), not the *content* of what he says when he speaks to God." The Greek translation in the Septuagint uses the expression *ou gar elalēsate enōpion mou alēthes ouden hōsper ho therapōn mou Iōb* (For they said nothing truthful before me [e.g., before my eyes; *ōps* = eye] as did my servant Job). For more on the language used in the Book of Job, see Cheney, *Dust* and Greenstein, "Invention of Language," especially 336–37.

32. See also Svartvik, *Textens tilltal*, 71–92.

33. Ps 145:18 (italics added).

individual's *sincere approach* that is the determining factor when meeting God. For example, Moses Mendelssohn's translation *die aufrichtig ihn anrufen* (those who honestly call on him) and the paraphrasing by David Kimhi (whose name is often shortened to *Radak*) that the Lord is near all those who call, regardless which people they belong to, if they turn to God in truth, such that mouth and heart speak the same language.[34] The Swedish Bible 2000 aligns with the second interpretation: "Herren är nära alla som ropar, alla som av hjärtat ropar till honom (the Lord is near all who call, all who call to him from their heart.)"

We could say that the account of Jacob at the ford of the Jabbok expresses that *he sees what no eye has seen,* that the description of Elijah on Mount Horeb is about *hearing what no ear has heard,* and that the Book of Job paints the portrait of a person whose *mouth and heart speak the same language,* expressing wholeheartedly the contents of the human innermost being. "But we speak," as Paul expresses the three-part idea in 1 Corinthians, "what no eye has seen, nor ear heard, nor the human heart conceived, what God has prepared for those who love him."[35]

The Cross and the Lynching Tree

We turn now to African American Christianity, to those who are the descendants of the millions of people "taking the form of a slave."[36] What can be learned from those who have not only worn the cross as a fine ornament around their throats but also, as Simon of Cyrene who carried the cross of Jesus, were forced to carry it on their backs?[37] If we truly wish to avoid developing theological models that relay a sanctioning of violence, a romanticizing of suffering, and a pacification of vulnerable people, then

34. Jospe, "Pluralism," 120.

35. 1 Cor 2:9. A more literal translation was selected here. Cf. how Popov summarizes the statements of the church fathers about human beings' notions of God, to *see* God and to *hear* words of God, in "Idea of Deification," 71.

36. Phil 2:7. The Greek word *doulos* means both "servant" and "slave." The crucifixion was a punishment intended for slaves and other people of low social standing (Latin *humiliores*). See Hengel, *Crucifixion,* 14: "the cruelest of all penalties" 34 and 51–63 (about crucifixion as *servile supplicium* [punishment of slaves]). See also Chapman, *Ancient Jewish.*

37. In the accounts of the Evangelists, Simon of Cyrene was forced by the Roman soldiers to carry the cross of Jesus. See Matt 27:32, Mark 15:21, and Luke 23:26 (however, not in John 19:17).

there is probably nothing more helpful than responding to those who have been subjected to violence and listening to those who suffer. There is every reason in the world to examine how African American Christianity has grappled with the troublesome Good Friday theologies.[38] How is the suffering and death of Jesus presented to those who have experienced so much of oppression in the forms of slavery, segregation, and discrimination? Matthew V. Johnson writes: "African American theology has a message not simply *for* African Americans but *from* African Americans to the whole of the Christian church and the world."[39]

In his choice of title, *The Cross and the Lynching Tree,* James H. Cone marks the striking similarity between the crucifixion of Jesus and the lynching of thousands of black people in the American South.[40]

> The lynching tree—so strikingly similar to the cross on Golgotha—should have a prominent place in American images of Jesus' death. But it does not. In fact, the lynching tree has no place in American theological reflection about Jesus' cross or in the proclamation of Christian churches about his Passion.[41]

Cone therefore asks, justifiably, how it can be that so few people see the parallels between the crucifixion and the lynchings.[42] Why have we not seen

38. Cone, *Cross,* 64: "White theologians do not normally turn to the black experience to learn about theology." For a presentation of African American history, see Hope Franklin and Am Moss Jr., *From Slavery to Freedom.*

39. Johnson, "Lord of the Crucified," 28.

40. The origin of the word "lynching" is probably from Charles Lynch (1736–96), but this is not confirmed. See Cone, *Cross,* 3–4. It is difficult to calculate the number of lynchings. Robert M. Franklin writes that there were more than a hundred per year. See "African American Pilgrimage," 169. Noel reports that more than 3,000 black people were lynched between the years of 1863 and 1963; see "Were You There?" *Passion of the Lord,* 48. Cone refers to a historical apology from the U.S. Senate, in which the number of lynchings was estimated to be around 5,000. See *Cross,* 99.

41. Cone, *Cross,* 31. In his book, Cone discusses some writers who did not note or expand upon the similarities between the cross and the lynching tree. It is actually not until p. 161 that he presents his main purpose, namely, to explore the similarities and their theological consequences. Because the body of the book ends on 166, he does not expand upon his argument. The most striking statement of the book must be on p. 112: "It is exceedingly doubtful if lynching could possibly exist under any other religion than Christianity."

42. Cone, *Cross,* 94: "Did it require such a leap of imagination to recognize the visual and symbolic overtones between the cross and the lynching tree, both places of execution in the ancient and modern worlds?" There are (a few) exceptions, however, including Edwin Taliaferro Wellford's book *Lynching of Jesus,* published in 1905; see Cone, *Cross,* 62–63.

the similarities between the one who was fastened to the trunk of the cross and all the ones who were hung from branches in the American South?

> Both the cross and the lynching tree were symbols of terror, instruments of torture and execution, reserved primarily for slaves, criminals, and insurrectionists—the lowest of the low in society. . . . Both were public spectacles, shameful events, instruments of punishment reserved for the most despised people in society.[43]

When we see and realize how similar the cross and lynching tree are, we avoid sentimentalizing the cross of Jesus by turning it into a magic talisman or reducing it to a mere religious symbol or an abstract theological concept.[44] Cone's book comes to terms with the theology that may preach the suffering of Christ but nonetheless is incapable of seeing and therefore neglects those who suffer today.

The song "Strange Fruit" was written in the early 1930s by Abel Meeropol, a Jewish teacher from New York who eventually changed his name to Lewis Allen. When he saw one of the photographs that were taken at many of these lynchings—and which were often printed as postcards and disseminated—he was horrified and wrote the song that was so often sung by Billie Holiday. "Southern trees bear strange fruit. *Blood on the leaves and blood at the root* . . . a strange and bitter crop." This song gives us a language to express the realization that there are excruciatingly many similarities between the crucifixion of Jesus and the lynchings. Jesus was strange fruit, too, and the opposite applies as well: Jesus is Lord of the crucified.[45]

These similarities pave the way for a feeling of nearness to Jesus. The identification swings in one direction and then the other like a pendulum. The New Testament accounts of Jesus' last days and hours make it possible for those who suffer to identify with him and feel his pain as their own. In the victimization and pain of Jesus, Africa American Christians have found a parallel to their own situations, which have been characterized by slavery, segregation, lynchings, and discrimination. Those who persecute, lash, and kill cannot seem to see what is apparent—yes, revealed—to those who are tormented, lacerated, killed, and more or less summarily judged.[46]

43. Cone, *Cross*, 31 and 161.

44. Cone, *Cross*, 108.

45. Cone, *Cross*, 120–21, and 158. See also Johnson, "Lord of the Crucified," 18; and Baker-Fletcher, *Passion of the Lord*, 113.

46. See also Cone, *Cross*, 75 and 159.

When Mel Gibson's film *The Passion of the Christ* was being debated, it emerged that Gibson truly meant to portray that the suffering of Jesus surpassed that which a human being was able to withstand.[47] A theology that portrays the suffering of Jesus as by definition overshadowing the suffering of others is rejected by JoAnn M. Terrell, among others. Why should it be theologically important that Jesus was whipped in a way that exceeded the whippings her slave ancestors had been subjected to repeatedly? Everyone who has seen the movie *Twelve Years a Slave* is likely to agree with her.[48] The point is not to compare suffering, but something completely different. The fundamental idea is not to compare but to *share*.

> God identifies with us in all manner of suffering and does not seek to supersede us in suffering either in quantity or quality, but to persuade us to stop inflicting suffering, once and for all, and to assure us that whatever we suffer, however determined evil is against us, we can and we will be redeemed.[49]

This idea is expressed already in the New Testament. The author of the Epistle to the Hebrews writes, "For we do not have a high priest who is unable to sympathize with our weaknesses, but we have one who in every respect has been tested as we are, yet without sin."[50] The word "sympathy" comes from the Greek *sym-pathein*, which literally means "to suffer with." The heavenly high priest has sympathy because he has suffered and suffers with those who suffer.

The pendulum swings back in the other direction. Not only is Jesus with them—they are also with him. There is, in African American tradition, a crucifixion theology that concludes with a summons. The motif of Christians being called to carry the cross of Jesus is tied to one specific person, namely the previously mentioned Simon of Cyrene.[51] In the Synoptic Gospels, this man from Cyrene, in today's Libya, was forced to carry the cross of Jesus. *The person who bears the burden of Jesus in the*

47. Mel Gibson interviewed by Peggy Noonan, reproduced in Svartvik, *Förundran*, 73. Cf. *Svenska psalmboken*, 142:1–4: "Jesus' pain was like none other's" (Swedish *Så som Jesu smärta var aldrig någons varit har*).

48. The film, directed by Steve McQueen, is based on the autobiographical novel of the same name by Solomon Northup, published in 1853.

49. Terrell, "What Manner," *Passion of the Lord*, 74.

50. Heb 4:15.

51. Cone, *Cross*, 82; and Terrell, "What Manner," 62.

most actual way in the New Testament comes from Africa.[52] Martin Luther King, speaking on May 22, 1967, describes the cross in a way that clearly expresses this. "It is not something that you *wear*. The cross is something that you *bear* and ultimately that you die on."[53]

Cross theology has been likened here to the swinging of a pendulum. In one direction, Christ in his suffering is with those who are afflicted. In the other, Christians are called to be in his place. They should, like the African Simon of Cyrene, carry the cross of Jesus. The cross may not explain everything in existence, but it is a symbol that leads to action.[54]

"This is . . . for you"

We return now to the basic question. What can the words of the Holy Communion, "This is . . . for you" mean to the individual human being today? This chapter closes therefore with a few thoughts on Holy Communion. Its international name is the Eucharist, from the Greek *eucharistia,* which means "thanksgiving." Communion comes from "community" (Latin *communio*), "mystery" (Greek *to mystērion*), or even "mystery of

52. That Simon came from Cyrene in what is now Libya is told in Matt 27:32, Mark 15:21, and Luke 23:26. It is much more difficult to determine if he was a Jew. In Mark 15:21, Simon is described as "the father of Alexander and Rufus." Some grave inscriptions found in Jerusalem on November 10, 1941 are therefore interesting. They date to the time before the fall of the Second Temple. "Alexander, [son of] Simon," "Alexander, [son] of Simon," and "[son?] of Alexander [in Greek lettering], and *Alek[h]sandros qrnyt* [in Hebrew lettering]." The Hebrew word *qrnyt* could mean "from Cyrene" (spelled incorrectly); see Avigad, "A Depository of Inscribed Ossuaries in the Kidron Valley." Simon was a common name among speakers of both Hebrew and Greek. There existed a large Jewish group from Cyrene. In a draft of a sermon from 1946, Fridrichsen outlines the theological implications of claiming that Simon was *not* a Jew. See *Fyrahanda sädesåker*, 263: "Under det att Israel [*sic*] korsfäster sin Messias bär en främling korset efter honom till Golgata (While Israel crucifies its Messiah, a stranger carries the cross after him to Golgotha). Försoningens universella syftning skymtar kanske fram redan i denna detalj i Kristi pinas historia (Here perhaps may already be glimpsed in this detail of the suffering of Christ the universal intent of reconciliation)."

53. Quoted in Cone, *Cross*, 84 (italics added). For an anthology of the writings and speeches of Martin Luther King, see Washington, ed., *Testament of Hope*. King has been accused of expressing things in a way that makes undeserved suffering sound like a kind of deliverance. At the same time, he emphasized that the Christian message has unavoidable consequences and should lead to action. See Demetrius K. Williams, "Identifying with the Cross," 107.

54. Gunton, *Actuality of Atonement*, 84.

mysteries."[55] The following is based on the five basic eucharistic motifs outlined by Geoffrey Wainwright in his article on the Eucharist in the *Oxford Companion to Christian Thought*.[56]

(a) The first motif is that *in the Eucharist, Christians meet the Living God*. If there is anything constructive in Christians' heartrending battles over Holy Communion doctrine, then it might be that almost all of them are about the way in which God is present in what is happening. In what way is God present in the bread and wine? This observation may serve as a reminder that the *divine presence* is a cornerstone of Christian theology. Matthew begins explicitly and ends implicitly with references to the divine presence. The Hebrew word *'immanuel* means "God [is] with us," and the Gospel ends with the words, "And remember, I am with you always, to the end of the age."[57] Similarly, Johannine theology emphasizes the importance of "remaining."[58] Communion hymns tend to be about the divine presence, about the holy and sanctifying presence.[59] For Christians, the Eucharist is a manifestation of divine presence in a world that is too often characterized by the absence of what we consider to be divine goodness. When the stranger leaves the two disciples in Emmaus, they still hold in their hands the bread that he shared with them.[60] *The Eucharist is the presence of that which seems absent.*

(b) Wainwright's second motif is that *the Eucharist is unavoidably related to the death of Jesus*. A large part of this book has been devoted to critically

55. The Greek word *eucharistein* means "to thank"; see 1 Thess 1:2: "We always give thanks to God" (*Eucharistoumen tō[i] Theō[i] pantote*). For the expression "mystery of mysteries," see Clément, "Introduktion till den ortodoxa kyrkans liv och lära," 23.

56. Wainwright, "Eucharist," *Oxford Companion to Christian Thought*, 214–17. Here, however, we will present and discuss them in a different order.

57. Matt 1:23 and 28:20. See also Isa 7:14.

58. E.g., John 15:1–10.

59. See *Svenska psalmboken*, 392:1f.: "Det helga bröd på altarbordet vilar som Jesus själv en gång i Betlehem. . . . Här krubban är—jag faller ned, tillbeder. . . . O, sakrament, som oss i nåd bereder att Gud, den evige, på jorden se (The holy bread rests on the altar as Jesus once lay in Bethlehem. . . . Here at the manger—I bow to pray. . . . O sacrament that mercifully prepares us on earth to see God everlasting)." This hymn combines two motifs. Jesus as the Word, the voice of God, and the Eucharist, as a sacrament of incarnation, the repast of the divine presence. In Muslim tradition, Jews and Christians are described as *ahl al-kitab*, "peoples of the book." Jews, as a people that strives to be true to God's revelation (*ha-Torah*), are certainly well described as being "of the *Book*," but should not Christians be called "of the *Word*," a people that wishes to follow the divine Word that "became flesh and lived among us" (John 1:14)?

60. Luke 24:31. See also Schreiter, *Ministry of Reconciliation*, 35 and 47.

examining destructive presentations of the crucifixion. How can we understand the relationship between the death of Jesus and the final meal shared with the disciples, between his crucifixion and the Christian Eucharist?

> Many Christians see the Holy Communion as the true center of the Christian worship service. Jesus invites them to Communion and to listen and learn from his words: "Do this is remembrance of me!" They are called upon to act a certain way: "Do *this* in remembrance of me!" Not, "Do *that* in remembrance of me!" The difference has been spelled out by S. Mark Heim, who lays specific emphasis on the word, "that."[61] Do not portray God as a bloodthirsty heavenly parent who demands the suffering and death of a son! Do not accuse anyone of the death of Jesus, do not torture, do not kill in the name of God! Do not do *that!* Instead, do *this* in remembrance of me, that which Christians do when they gather to worship: thank God, sing hymns praising God, share food and drink, bread and wine. In this way the crucifixion in Christian Communion points away from violence.[62]

This reasoning, from my previous book *Amazement and Anticipation*, can now be expanded upon. In the Jewish Passover meal, there is an element called *ha-maggid* or *maggid* that is part of the Passover story. In celebrating Passover, people recount God's good deeds in remembrance of what God did for the Jewish people by leading them out of Egypt. The introduction to the ceremony is in Aramaic, an indication that it is an ancient element of the Passover meal.[63] The person who is leading raises the unleavened bread and says, *ha lachma 'ania* (This is the bread of affliction), which is a reference to Deuteronomy 16:3 (Hebrew *lechem 'oni*). Now, it just so happens that the word for the first person singular pronoun in both Hebrew (*ani*) and Aramaic (*ana*) are very similar to the word that describes unleavened bread. So, the Aramaic *ha lachma ana* and the Hebrew *ha-lechem ani* are a likening of oneself with the bread of affliction: I am this bread, or This

61. Heim, "Saved," 224. See also his monograph, *Saved from Sacrifice*.

62. Svartvik, *Förundran*, 75. Heim has been influenced by the writings of Girard, expressing that the crucifixion of Jesus should be seen as the end of an accusatory scapegoat theology. Yet in Heim we find much more self-critical conclusions, that is, that *Christians* should, in the name of cross theology, refrain from accusing *others.* In sum, Girard tends to describe the Christian faith as the answer to the problems that the religious traditions of offering create. Heim instead draws attention to there being something problematic with Christian cross theologies. For Heim, the word "offering" means only "victim."

63. For more information on the Jewish Passover meal, see Martola, *Kommentar till påskhaggadan*.

bread is me. Imagine if this tradition were the source of what we today call the Words of Institution. If so, it must be one of the most widespread and yet most unknown alliterations in world history.[64] Might Jesus, just a few hours before his arrest in Gethsemane, be referring to the liturgy of the Passover ceremony as way of expressing his own affliction?

The Eucharist is unavoidably tied to the death of Jesus. The liturgy becomes a way for Christians to remember when they gather that they should do "this" in remembrance of Jesus: thank God, sing God's praise, share food and drink, bread and wine. They should not do *that,* but *this.* The celebration of Holy Communion is a way to remember the life and teachings of Jesus. It is not only about remembering him correctly, but also in a way that is healing.[65] The words "do *this* in remembrance of me" is an indication of how this remembrance can be expressed. The crucifixion then becomes something that, in the Communion service, points away from violence—and neither sanctions violence nor romanticizes suffering.

(c) A third point is that *the Eucharist is part of Christian community as a whole.* In 1 Corinthians—most likely the oldest existing text on the Eucharist—Paul addresses the internal conflict among Christians in Corinth. He writes that their divisiveness went against the spirit of the Eucharist.[66] Reconciliation and transformation are a large part of interhuman relations. The teaching of the Sermon on the Mount, to reconcile first with one's fellow humans before offering at the temple, is still practiced in Judaism today.[67] During the ten days between the Jewish New Year celebration of Rosh Ha-shanah and Yom Kippur, many conversations take place, letters are written, telephone calls are made, and many emails are sent. The individual's relationship with God may not and cannot be isolated from the relationship with other human beings. Many of Jesus' parables emphasize the way these two relationships—that is, with God

64. Many thanks to Abraham Zvi Schwarcz (*Shav-Aretz*) for stimulating talks on this topic. For comparisons between Jewish and Christian liturgy, see Hoffman, "Jewish and Christian Liturgy," 175–89.

65. Cf. 1 Cor 11:26. Cf. the three aspects delineated by Volf in *End of Memory*, 93: "'Remember truthfully!' 'Remember therapeutically!' and 'Learn from the past!'"

66. 1 Cor 11:17–34. See also 1 Cor 10:16–17.

67. Cf. Matt 5:23–26, especially v. 24: "So when you are offering your gift at the altar, if you remember that your brother or sister has something against you, leave your gift there before the altar and go; *first* be reconciled to your brother or sister, and *then* come and offer your gift" (italics added). For further viewpoints, see Göran Larsson, *Tid för Gud*, 102–5.

and with other human beings—are integrated. Perhaps most clear is the parable of the unforgiving servant who has an enormous debt forgiven yet refuses to forgive the small debt another slave owes him.[68] Divine and human relations are also integrated in the Lord's Prayer. "And forgive us our debts, as we also have forgiven our debtors."[69]

(d) For his fourth point, Wainwright writes that *the Eucharist, expressed as bread and wine, is interrelated with the relationships of our world.* The Eucharist is a liturgical reminder that when bread is divided, everyone eats. To live eucharistically is to hunger and thirst for righteousness.[70] In the book *Eucharist and Torture,* William T. Cavanaugh argues that Communion can be the church's proper response to injustice, particularly torture. After the Last Supper, Jesus was in the hands of Rome's powerful men, who tortured and killed him. Communion theology is therefore unavoidably related to a number of ethical questions. How should the followers of Jesus relate to the power establishment? What is the relationship between ethics and theology? How is sacramental theology related to social ethics? In *Eucharist and Torture,* Cavanaugh looks most closely at the situation in Chile during the time of General Augusto Pinochet, 1973 to 1990. Cavanaugh argues that the theology of the Communion cannot be isolated from its consequences. Holy Communion is an expression of the community that Christians feel and create together. The Eucharist—the element of Christian liturgy that most clearly relates to the death of Jesus—can thus be a response to oppression.[71] Instead of disarming believers by sanctioning violence and romanticizing suffering, Holy Communion can be a voice for the people of our world who are suffering.

(e) Finally, Wainwright highlights that *the Eucharist is eschatological.* It is an event that points beyond itself. It is a foretaste of the future, a future that breathes hope and faith. The Eucharist is a premonition of a reconciled and transformed world.[72] Haddon Willmer raises the importance of this

68. Matt 18:23–35. The first slave had been enormously in debt (ten thousand talents), whereas the other slave only owed him a hundred denarii.

69. Matt 6:12. Luke 11:4 does not use the financial term "debts" (*ta opheilēmata*) but rather the more theological term, "sins" (*tas hamartias*).

70. Matt 5:6. Cf. Luke 6:21.

71. Cavanaugh, *Torture and Eucharist*, e.g., 273: "Opposition to the powers and principalities of the world is written into the very narrative of the death and resurrection of Jesus Christ which is commemorated in the Eucharist."

72. Cf. Schreiter, *Ministry of Reconciliation*, 69.

perspective toward the future for interhuman relations—and thereby also reconciliation and transformation.

> When forgiving is effective, wrong is remembered, but no longer sets the agenda for the future or consumes people's lives.[73]

Renewal and Revival

The future is the great challenge, but we have to live in the here and now and interpret it with the help of the past—that is, using experience, learning, and insight that fosters and forms us as human beings. At the root of the Hebrew word *teshuvah* and the Greek *metanoia* is a transformative change of heart and, especially, a spiritual conversion. Both words have to do with renewed direction in life. The person who repents changes view, gets a new perspective—and sees life in a new way. Willmer defines repentance as being less about turning away from the past and more about turning toward the future.

> Jesus invited people to repent by welcoming and living in accord with the coming Kingdom of God; repentance was less from past sin, more towards the future. This way of thinking does not minimize repentance, but it does prevent its being turned into a moral precondition dispensing the forgiver from risking the generous pioneering inventiveness of forgiving. It obviates the fashionable pious error which sees forgiving as holy impotence rather than the exercise of power to effect liberating and humanizing change.[74]

In sum, both the resurrection of Christ and human repentance indicates a direction and shows a way: reconciliation and transformation are movements forward. An unavoidable aspect of the process of reconciliation is this forward-looking perspective. We have wounds, inside and out, from the past, but when we look forward, hopefully we can see that we are more than our wounds.[75] This is one of the possibilities of being human, says Annicka Lindberg, that of not remaining in disgrace.

> Christian life is a continual return to God. "We fall and we rise"—even the Desert Fathers described their lives this way. No one lives

73. Willmer, "Forgiveness," 245.
74. Willmer, "Forgiveness," 246.
75. Cf. Patton, "Foreword," 8: "None of us is only the sum of our wounds."

> without committing sin, but the human experience includes the possibility of recovery. A human being can rise and repent—in metanoia—do penance.[76]

What is it that makes it possible for the individual human being to regain grace? Christians through the ages have sought the answer to this question in the resurrection of Christ. Easter, the day of the resurrection, is the day of the Christian *festum festorum*, the celebration of all celebrations, the holiest of holy days. The message of Easter is that human beings, as Anders Piltz writes, "with the resurrection are . . . restored, raised, and uplifted to royal dignity."[77] It is often said that every Sunday is an Easter Day. So, we should be able to preach this in every Christian worship service: a restored, raised, and uplifted humanity. The last chapter of this book will be devoted to the Christian belief in the resurrection and its consequences.

76. From Lindberg, "Några drag i den ortodoxa kyrkans liv," 11.

77. Piltz, *Som regnet och snön*, 79.

9

Transformation as the Central Motif

THIS BOOK BEGINS WITH the first word of its title and has reached its last: *transformation*. The transformational consequences of belief in the resurrection for the Christian approach to life will be discussed in this closing chapter.[1] Naturally, much can be said on this topic, but we limit ourselves here to three aspects: (a) the crucial meaning of the resurrection; (b) its consequences; and (c) undesirable side effects.

The Message of Christ and the Resurrection

When Paul preaches on the Christian faith in Athens, according to Acts of the Apostles, some listeners believe he is "a proclaimer of foreign divinities." Luke explains, "This was because he was telling the good news about Jesus and the resurrection."[2] It may be that this Christian speech about Jesus (in Greek the name *Iēsous* takes the masculine form) and the resurrection (*hē anastasis* takes the feminine) was taken as a lesson on a couple of gods: the god Jesus and the goddess Anastasis! In other words, early Christian professions of faith emphasized the resurrection to such a degree that it may have been misunderstood as an independent divine being. This comical misunderstanding is actually revealing, because it indicates the importance of the resurrection for early Christian theology.[3] In the beginning, there was the resurrection. In his *Catechetical Homilies*, Cyril of Jerusalem (ca. 310–386) spells out the relationship between the death of Jesus and the resurrection:

1. This chapter is based on and develops ideas that are included in chapter 7 of my book *Förundran*, 103–18.

2. Acts 17:18.

3. For this interpretation, see Edvin Larsson, *Apostlagärningarna 13–20*, 379.

> I confess the Cross, because I know of the Resurrection; for if, after being crucified, He had remained as He was, I had not perchance confessed it, for I might have concealed both it and my Master; but now that the Resurrection has followed the Cross, I am not ashamed to declare it.[4]

Cyril sharpens our perception of the danger of presenting the crucifixion of Jesus in a way isolates it from the Christian belief in the resurrection. The question is if *anastasis* is at all needed in a theology that claims that the death of Jesus is *all*-important. Has there been a tendency in Western Christian theology to overemphasize the message of Good Friday to the degree that the crucifixion has come to overshadow other—equally important—aspects of the Christian faith? If yes, then does the Eastern Orthodox tradition, with its emphasis on *anastasis* have something significant to contribute? In this chapter, we will explore Eastern Orthodox theology.

The fact is that some presentations of Jesus' death shift the focus completely away from the resurrection. If the death of Jesus alone could bring us reconciliation, it is difficult to understand or explain why preaching the news of the resurrection should be so important to the first Christians. Ultimately, an overemphasis on the events of Good Friday renders the resurrection irrelevant.[5] This observation is also made by Vigen Guroian:

> If one presses the logic of this contemporary piety of the Cross, the Resurrection . . . becomes unnecessary, for on Holy Friday Jesus accomplishes all that was needed in order that humankind might inherit eternal life. . . . Ironically, this piety of the Cross could not have come about but for the early church's conviction that the Resurrection is, indeed, the culmination of the Passion story.[6]

Naturally, the death of Jesus should not be made theologically unimportant; it simply must not be isolated from Christian resurrection doctrine. The concept of incarnation should be allowed to incorporate the entire chain of events: birth, life, teaching, death—and resurrection. In the words of the Nicene creed:

> Who for us men and for our salvation, came down from heaven, and was incarnate by the Holy Spirit of the Virgin Mary, and was

4. Cyril of Jerusalem, *Catechetical Lectures 13–23*, Lecture 13.4.

5. Belousek, *Atonement*, 111: "The cross is the sum and substance of God's work, penal substitution claims, leaving the resurrection as inessential and inconsequential. The Evangelists and Apostles, we shall see, tell the story differently."

6. Guroian, *Melody*, 94.

> made man. *And* he was crucified for us under Pontius Pilate, and suffered, and was buried. *And the third day he rose again, according to the scriptures.*

Emphasis on the Teaching, Death, or Resurrection of Jesus?

At the risk of oversimplifying a multitude of opinions, we could say that liberal Christians are eager to talk about Jesus' *radical teaching* about the kingdom of God, while conservative Christians are more likely to emphasize the long-term influence of the *suffering and death of Jesus on the cross.* In interpretations that emphasize the events of Good Friday, it is not unusual to find the belief that human beings should be affected and upset by the suffering and death of Jesus because he died in the place of sinners.

Relating the suffering of others to one's own suffering is undeniably important, but this motif should not be allowed to overshadow another motif that is considerably more prominent in early Christian writings, namely that it is knowledge of the resurrection that truly, fundamentally, transforms Christians. The one day of the Church Year that would be associated with *transformation* in early Christian faith and thought would not be Good Friday; it would be Easter. An example of this view can be found in Ephesians.

> I pray that the God of our Lord Jesus Christ, the Father of glory, may give you a spirit of wisdom and revelation as you come to know him, so that, with the eyes of your heart enlightened, you may know what is the hope to which he has called you, what are the riches of his glorious inheritance among the saints, and what is the immeasurable greatness of his power for us who believe, *according to the working of his great power. God put this power to work in Christ when he raised him from the dead* and seated him at his right hand in the heavenly places.[7]

In short, the first Christians' belief in the resurrection was what made Jesus important. The intrinsic power in his *teaching* gained preeminence because of the resurrection. The importance of his *death* was also revealed in light of his resurrection.

7. Eph 1:18–20. See also 2 Cor 13:4: "For he was crucified in weakness but lives by the power of God. For we are weak in him, but in dealing with you we will live with him by the power of God. Examine yourselves to see whether you are living in the faith."

A Guest and a Stranger

The Greek word *xenos* means both guest and stranger. The word *xenophobia* means a fear and hatred of strangers or foreigners or of anything that is strange or foreign. The Greek word *philoxenia*—or just *xenia*—means an act of hospitality and welcome.[8] (In Swedish, interestingly, when guests are expected, they are called "strangers.")

Overemphasizing the events of Good Friday can lead to the crucifixion of Jesus being reduced—even distorted, warns Rowan Williams—into an apologetic argument defending one's personal beliefs. Jesus' cross can be changed into a sword in hand to use against others. To refer back to the previous chapter, he writes of a Good Friday theology that both romanticizes suffering and uses the cross for one's own profit.

> To use the cross of Jesus as a vehicle for making sense of my suffering, a symbolic mediation which gives my experience back to me newly located and interpreted, is not necessarily an illegitimate step to take. But symbolic mediation is a slippery matter: if my interpretation simply stops at this point, I risk turning the cross itself into a defense of my position, a legitimation. This is how the cross can be made to serve an ideological purpose. God is identified with *my* cause, because he is identified with *my* suffering: the cross is the banner of my ego—or the banner of a collective ego. If I suffer I am in the right, because God "endorses" my pain. . . . To stop with Good Friday is to see the crucified simply as reflecting back to me my own condition, and even to remember the crucified, in the superficial sense, can merely leave us with a martyr for our cause. . . . So Easter does carry with it the possibility of change in the individual and in humanity; but that possibility depends upon understanding the cross first of all as "not mine."[9]

"The theme of the familiar stranger, the alien friend" in the Gospels and in the Christian tradition is important to Rowan Williams.[10] He argues that the cross ceases to be an ideological weapon only when we see and understand that the cross belongs to both the familiar stranger and the strange friend. The people who went to the grave to honor a martyr found an empty grave, Williams observes, but the two who were walking

8. For more on these concepts, see Svartvik, "Introduction" *Religious Stereotyping*, 15. See also de Béthune, *Interreligious Hospitality* and Moyaert, *Fragile Identities*.

9. Williams, *Resurrection*, 70, 71, and 73.

10. Williams, *Resurrection*, 67.

to Emmaus and invited a stranger to share a meal were surprised to discover Jesus in their company. Williams argues that this is a fundamental part of the resurrection story in the New Testament, "this theme of otherness, the unrecognizability, of the risen Jesus."[11] In short, the meeting on the road to Emmaus with the Resurrected One was a meeting with a familiar *stranger* and a *strange* friend. Even when Christ himself is a guest of Christians, he remains a stranger, mysterious and unfathomable. It is the meeting with the risen Jesus that truly changes them. This chapter therefore wishes to raise a third, early Christian, motif: *the resurrection* as expressed in Eastern Orthodox Christianity. Jesus' resurrection gives *life,* renewed and transformed, and in abundance.[12] We will now briefly consider two concepts that have to do with human beings (often called "partakers of divinity") and the world ("the eighth day").

Partakers of Divinity

The Second Epistle of Peter holds the oldest explicit suggestion that it might be possible for human beings to partake of divinity.[13] While Western theology has highlighted the many faults and limitations of human nature, Eastern Christian theologians have more consistently pursued the approach of the New Testament to consider the goal of humanity to be *theōsis*, "becoming godlike." What is meant by *theōsis*—and what does it have to do with *anastasis?*

Before answering this question, it is necessary to become familiar with a few more terms. The first concept is that of God's "being" or "essence" (Greek *ousia*), which is inaccessible and yet unavoidable. "Thy name so greatly desired and constantly proclaimed, none is able to say what it is," writes Symeon, known as the New Theologian (949–1022).[14] However, it is just as true that God works in the world, and that the will of God is revealed

11. Rowan Williams, *Resurrection*, 67. Cf. Svartvik, *Förundran*, 143–45.

12. Cf. John 10:10.

13. 2 Pet 1:4. The Greek expression is *theias koinōnoi physeōs*. See also Matt 5:48; John 10:34 (which cites Ps 82:6); 1 Cor 15:28; 2 Cor 3:18, 4:16; Eph 4:24; Phlm 3:21; 1 John 3:2. For further views on the context of 2 Pet 1:4, see Starr, *Sharers in Divine Nature*. For more on *theōsis* theology, see Mantzaridis, *Deification of Man*; Nellas, *Deification in Christ*; Finlan and Kharlamov, eds., *Theōsis*; Collins, *Partaking in Divine Nature*, and, Kharlamov, ed., *Theōsis*.

14. Quoted in Lossky, *Mystical Theology*, 160. For a presentation of Symeon, see Halldorf, "Symeon: teolog i Ande och sanning," 7–20.

through *energeia* (action, energy) and *dynamis* (potentiality).[15] Though inaccessible in being, God is nonetheless revealed through *energeia*—but as if in a mirror.[16] *Energeia* is that which is on "our side" of the divine essence, which is "beyond" human belief and thought.

Two other concepts also belong together, namely *sarkōsis* (incarnation; cf. *sarx*, flesh, body, human being) and the previously mentioned *theōsis* (deification; cf. *Theos*, God). These two words, *sarkōsis* and *theōsis*, implicate and embrace either other, as is evident in the famous expression used by many church fathers, though most often associated with Athanasius of Alexandria: "For he became man that we might become divine; and he revealed himself through a body that we might receive an idea of the invisible Father."[17] Another expression that allows *sarkōsis* and *theōsis* to cooperate, if perhaps more difficult to grasp, is that humans will remain created beings though mercifully included in divine nature (*theōsis*), as Christ remains divine though made human through incarnation (*sarkōsis*).[18] A third way to express it is that human beings, through divine grace, become that which Christ is by nature.[19]

We see here how Eastern Orthodox theology describes God's revelation and humanity's calling more or less without dependence upon the events of Good Friday. God became human (*sarkōsis*) so that human beings could become divine (*theōsis*). The suffering and death of Jesus on Good Friday are *part* of this, of course, but *sarkōsis* clearly comprises his whole life. His resurrection is described as a victory over death, baptism as the beginning of the resurrection, a way out of the labyrinth of death.[20] Lossky refers to the Pauline statements in 1 Corinthians. "The last enemy to be destroyed is death." "Death has been swallowed up in victory. Where, O death, is your victory? Where, O death, is your sting?"[21] In short, Holy Week cannot be separated from the message of Easter (*anastasis*), which

15. See Lossky, *Mystical Theology*, 70–73 and 86.

16. Cf. 1 Cor 13:12. Cf. the *ousia–energeia* dialectic with the *Deus absconditus* (the hidden God)–*Deus revelatus* (God revealed) pair of concepts.

17. Athanasius of Alexandria, *Contra Gentes* and *De Incarnatione*, 269. See also Lossky, *Mystical Theology*, 134. See also Stendahl, *Energy for Life*, 82.

18. Lossky, *Mystical Theology*, 87. On p. 138 he refers to Theophylact of Ohrid (1100s) who said that the Word remained what it was, yet at the same time, what it was not.

19. Lossky, *Mystical Theology*, 126.

20. Lossky, *Mystical Theology*, 136, 152–53 ("This victory over death is first of all declared in the Resurrection of the Lord") and 179.

21. 1 Cor 15:26 and 54–55. Cf. Isa 25:8 and Hos 13:14.

belongs to the mystery of incarnation (*sarkōsis*), which is described as "love of humanity" (*philanthrōpia*).[22] Here is a theological world that strives to do justice to both God's inscrutable being and the New Testament claim that human beings can be "participants of the divine nature."[23]

The Eighth Day

There is a risk of *marginalizing* the belief in Christian resurrection by preaching the events of Good Friday at the expense of the message of Easter morning. There is also a risk of *trivializing* it by reducing it to just another apologetic argument to convince oneself, basically, Jesus rose from the dead, so I am right, and you are wrong! Remembering what Sunday meant in early Christian liturgy and theology helps us avoid this kind of marginalization and trivialization.[24]

(a) Sunday is the *first day of the Creation* as described in Genesis. "And there was evening and there was morning, the first day."[25] Creation theology should always be integrated into the Christian faith. The Christian message cannot be made independently of the welfare of the world. Even less should it be contrasted to this world. A sense of wonder at the creation encourages a feeling of duty for its stewardship. In our times, human responsibility for the stewardship of the earth is becoming increasingly tangible, even urgent.

(b) Christians all over the world worship on Sunday, because it is *the day of resurrection.*[26] All four Evangelists write that it is on the first day of the week, Sunday, that they sorrowfully discover that the tomb is empty.[27] Already during the time of the New Testament, Christians gathered to

22. See Lossky, *Mystical Theology*, 139.

23. 2 Pet 1:4. This *theōsis* is completed first in the coming world; see Lossky, *Mystical Theology*, 196.

24. Cf. Moss's observation that Christian martyrdom is seen as an argument for the resurrection, *Myth of Persecution*, 23.

25. Gen 1:5; the events of the whole day are described in verses 3–5.

26. With few exceptions, Sunday is the Christian day of worship. Two alternatives are the Seventh Day Adventists, founded in 1863, and growing religious movements that are strongly influenced by Jewish belief and tradition (such as the Shabbat and kashruth [the dietary laws]). For more viewpoints of the Shabbat as a Jewish and/or Christian day of worship, see Eskenazi, Harrington, and Shea, eds., *Sabbath*.

27. Matt 28:1; Mark 16:2; Luke 24:1; John 20:1.

celebrate the Lord's Day (Greek *hē kyriakē hēmera*).[28] The Didache writings call upon readers to gather on the Day of the Lord to "break bread and give thanks," that is, to celebrate Holy Communion.[29]

(c) Sunday is also called "the eighth day." In the Epistle of Barnabas, it is expressed in an interesting way. "Therefore, we also celebrate with gladness the eighth day, in which Jesus rose from the dead."[30] Jesus' resurrection is not conceived as a wonder like the miracles attributed to him in the Gospels. Instead, the resurrection is interpreted as an eschatological manifestation, *a foretaste of the future.* Every Sunday is an Easter Sunday in that sense. Every Sunday is a foretaste of that which one day shall be.[31] In the words of the Swedish burial hymn, "When eternity's Easter dawns over Earth's graves, raise us in grace to eternal life."[32] It is interesting, when we think of the eighth day, that a reclining number eight, the lemniscate, symbolizes infinity.[33]

For these three reasons, Christians all over the world celebrate Christian worship service every Sunday. Every Sunday gives reason to *wonder* at creation, *proclaim* the resurrection of Jesus, and experience a *foretaste* of an altered and altering future.

These three motifs are expressed in the liturgy of the Armenian Church when the first seventeen verses of the Gospel of John (the Prologue) are read on the eighth day after Easter. The Prologue to the Gospel of John uses the language of the creation from Genesis to describe the incarnation. "In the beginning was the Word. . . . And the Word became flesh and lived among us, and we have seen his glory, the glory as of a father's only son, full of grace and truth."[34]

Is Sunday then primarily a day of rest? That it is, *also,* for an infinite number of Christians for whom it is primarily a day of resurrection and

28. See Acts 20:7; 1 Cor 16:2; Rev 1:10. Interestingly, in Gos. Pet. 35 and 50, the idea is used in the description of what happened at the grave of Jesus on the first day of the week.

29. Did. 14.1. The Greek verb *eucharistein* is the root of the international name Eucharist for Holy Communion. The Didache makes use of the cryptic expression *kata kyriakēn de kyriou* (on the Lord's [day] of the Lord).

30. Barn. 15.9.

31. Lossky, *Mystical Theology*, 106 and 220.

32. *Den svenska kyrkohandboken*, 223.

33. The word "lemniscate" comes from the Latin *lemniscus* (ribbon).

34. John 1:1 and 14. For the scriptural readings of the Armenian Church, see Guroian, *Melody*, 22.

a day to look ahead. Jewish Shabbat and Christian Sunday—the two holy days can be *compared*, not for *competition*, but for *contemplation*. These two Bible-reading communities, Judaism and Christianity, gather energy for renewal and transformation in different ways. For Jews, the Shabbat is a day of rest, a temple raised in time, and a foretaste of heavenly life. For Christians, Sunday is a day of resurrection and transformation, a foretaste of all that has come and gone and will someday be reborn.[35] Sunday is both the week's first and eighth day: the day of creation in the beginning of time, in the midst of time, and in the future. The Jewish Shabbat is the seventh and last day of the week, the day God rested after all was done.[36] Jews and Christians do not need to compete about which day is more correct or important: Jews celebrate the Shabbat as a reminder of the covenant between God and Israel. Christians celebrate Sunday as a manifestation of the resurrection of Christ from the dead. Describing Christian Sunday as a replacement for—or worse, freedom from—Jewish Shabbat means taking neither of the two religious traditions seriously.[37]

The Reconciliatory Power of the Resurrection

Now we are ready to discuss the implications of the resurrection for reconciliation. Is it the Christian belief in the resurrection, more so than in Jesus' death, that is transforming? The reconciliatory and transformational purport of the resurrection is emphasized in *The Ministry of Reconciliation*, by Robert J. Schreiter. The reconciliation theology he describes is primarily based on the New Testament accounts of the resurrection. The doctrine of the resurrection, he argues, is crucial to Christian understanding of reconciliation and transformation. The New Testament accounts of the disciples' meetings with the risen Jesus provide us with a key to interpreting how human beings can manage a violent past and start to build a new future and a renewed community.[38] We will limit ourselves to three standpoints.

35. On the idea of the Shabbat being a temple raised in time, see Heschel, *Sabbath*, 13–24.

36. Cf. Gen 2:2f.

37. Cf. the lectionary of *Den svenska psalmboken* on the theme of "Freedom in Christ," with three scripture readings on the sabbath (Exod 23:10–12, Mark 2:23–28, and Luke 13:10–17). Can the thinking behind this be anything but the odd idea that Christian faith frees human beings from celebrating Jewish Shabbat?

38. Schreiter, *Ministry of Reconciliation*, "might just hold the key to hope" (ibid., vi), and "coming to terms with a violent history, and of building the beginnings of a new

(a) *Jesus reveals himself to the disciples as they needed to see him.* This is primary, and an observation that Schreiter often makes. Each meeting with the risen Jesus mends relations, confirms trust, and heals broken hearts.[39] This is well expressed in the story of the disciples walking to Emmaus in the final chapter of Luke.[40] Two disciples were walking from Jerusalem to Emmaus, wondering at the rumors about Jesus rising from the dead. A stranger joins them and they converse as they travel. Eventually they invite the stranger to a meal. When they break bread together, they see it is Jesus! Schreiter quotes from the previously cited book by Rowan Williams on the resurrection. Williams argues that Easter happens when people no longer see Jesus as a dead friend but as a living stranger.[41]

(b) *Remembrance is important.* The transformation is not about *what* we remember, but *how* we remember. That means it is important to not forget. Reconciliation is not about forgetting what happened—how could that ever be possible?!—but about a transformation. "*In forgiving we do not forget, we remember in a different way.*"[42] To erase from our memories the things others have done to us would be to eradicate essential parts of who and what we are. But we can try to remember in another way after having gone through a reconciliation process.[43] This is why the New Testament resurrection accounts are so important, writes Schreiter: After having met the risen Jesus, the disciples remember the death of Jesus in a different way, in a new way, and in a changed way. The suffering is not forgotten, but the memory of it is changed. He uses the word *transfiguration* to describe this change. What comes to mind are the descriptions in the Synoptic Gospels of the transfiguration of Jesus that, according to tradition, took place on Mount Tabor in Galilee. He is transfigured right in front of the disciples, and they see him as he really is.[44] Or does it happen

---

humanity and a new community" (ibid., 6).

39. Schreiter, *Ministry of Reconciliation*, 48 and 89.

40. Luke 24:13–35. It is generally believed that Emmaus in the time of the Bible was located where Abu Ghosh lies today.

41. Rowan Williams, *Resurrection*, 74: "[Easter] occurs when we find in Jesus not a dead friend, but a living stranger." For further viewpoints, see Schreiter, *Ministry of Reconciliation*, 49. For a presentation of Williams's theology, see Myers, *Christ the Stranger*.

42. Schreiter, *Ministry of Reconciliation*, 66. See also Volf, *End of Memory*, 93.

43. Schreiter, *Ministry of Reconciliation*, 17–18, 66–67, 98–99, 102, 105, 111–12, 114.

44. See Matt 17:1–13; Mark 9:2–13; Luke 9:28–36. *Beit Tavor* (House of Tabor) is the Hebrew name of the building that houses the Swedish Theological Institute in Jerusalem. For a brief history, see Göran Larsson, *Fönster mot Gud*, 118–23. See also Holmquist,

as Vladimir Lossky argues is more likely, namely that the disciples change, and can now see who he was?

> The Transfiguration was not a phenomenon circumscribed in time and space; Christ underwent no change at that moment, even in His human nature, but a change occurred in the awareness of the apostles, who for a time received the power to see their Master as He was, resplendent in the eternal light of His Godhead.[45]

In short, the past should not be forgotten, writes Schreiter, but the memory of what happened can be changed, allowing the person remembering to be reconciled and transformed.

(c) *The perspective is forward-looking.* An essential idea of his book is that reconciliation is not about a return to status quo ante (the situation that existed previously).[46] It is not a question of returning to a previous state of affairs, of restoring, but instead of taking a giant step *forward*, not backward. That is why the events of Holy Week and the message of Easter are so relevant to his book on reconciliation. It is a question not of returning to the past but of turning to a completely new future. Reconciliation transports us to new places.[47] He calls it "coming to terms with a concrete past and working toward a different future within the constraints . . . of the context."[48] The essential thing is to make sure the future does not repeat the past.[49] "Forgiveness and reconciliation should thus be considered a process of reconstructing the moral order that is more healthy than punishment," he quotes José Zalaquett as saying.[50]

Schreiter's book reminds us how limited and misguided it is for Christians either to fight over the way in which Jesus' death—isolated from all else—is reconciliatory, or to reduce resurrection doctrine to an apologetic argument. Especially valuable in Schreiter's book is that he pays close attention to, sorts out, and expands upon the wealth of wisdom in the New Testament accounts of the resurrection. In these accounts, it is the meeting

---

Mötesplats Jerusalem and Sjögren, *Det var en gång en vallareman*, especially 181–201.

45. Lossky, *Mystical Theology*, 223.

46. Schreiter, *Ministry of Reconciliation*, 18.

47. Schreiter, *Ministry of Reconciliation*, 30–31. "Reconciliation always takes us to a new place. It does not simply transport us back to where we had been before the trauma occurred. . . . Knowing that one has been brought to a new place."

48. Schreiter, *Ministry of Reconciliation*, 105.

49. Schreiter, *Ministry of Reconciliation*, 113.

50. José Zalaquett, quoted in Schreiter, *Ministry of Reconciliation*, 111–12.

with the risen Jesus that reconciles and transforms, heals and uplifts. The wounds are visible in Jesus' hands, and we wounded human beings also carry scars of difficult experiences and painful memories, but we need to remember them in a different way.

This chapter's third and last task is to draw attention to and question a problematic tendency, namely, describing the death and resurrection of Jesus as *the absolute end* of something undesirable: with the death and resurrection of Jesus we abolish or banish someone or something we find difficult or painful. We could call this a paradigmatic interpretation. It is easy to understand how this way of thinking might arise. "It is finished"—these words in the Gospel of John echo in the ears of many Bible readers when this question is raised.[51] However, this view is problematic and needs to be looked at more closely. It is important to note that sometimes *we seem to talk about transformation in an incorrect or at least incomplete way.* We risk then making the mistake of spreading clichés that are neither historically nor theologically supported.

In the essay, "Framför en bokhylla (Standing before the Bookcase)," Frans G. Bengtsson describes his great love of reading, but also the type of literature he cannot read.

> I can now read almost everything that is written in a more or less human way and that has content . . . but there are exceptions that I will never manage, like a hungry person who sickens at the thought of eel or reacts to mussels. I cannot read . . . solemn investigations of everyday subjects, expressed popularly as "we live (understood: unlike any other time in history) in a time of great change."[52]

One cannot help thinking of Bengtsson's "we live in a time of great change" when we look at how the crucifixion and resurrection are sometimes presented. Good Friday and Easter are popularly presented as a time of great change, with distinct before-and-after pictures. Much space has already been devoted in this book to the thought of divine wrath being diverted because of the death of Jesus, but there are several other

51. John 19:30. In the radio broadcast of a worship service on March 28, 1955, Hugo Odeberg said that the Greek word *tetelestai* (which is usually translated as "it is finished") primarily meant "the last, tormented sigh of death, it is the sigh of death, the only words, 'The End.'" See the transcript in *Svenska Morgonbladet* of March 29. Only afterward, in "This word's deepest and most complete meaning" is there any reference to "the great act of salvation is complete." Cf. Rom 10:4: "Christ is the culmination [Greek *telos*] of the law."

52. Bengtsson, *Sällskap för en eremit*, 248–49.

paradigmatic interpretations, including that Jesus, through his death and resurrection, eliminated the Jewish law, Jewish offering rites in Jerusalem, Jewish religion—even religion in general. What unites all these catchphrases is that the death and resurrection of Jesus make possible a radical break with the past. There is therefore an impending risk of an anachronistic approach being used. The fact is that two thousand years ago, Christianity did not introduce freedom for slaves, equality between men and women, or brotherhood and sisterhood between heterosexual and homosexual people—or whatever example we choose.[53]

The Greatest Friend of Truth Is Time

Social change, and especially change in social values, takes times. That is why the paradigmatic explanations of the meaning of the cross are so problematic. It takes time for something that is fundamentally different to be introduced and win the hearts and trust of people. Revolutionary change, almost without exception, has a long prehistory. One example is the abolition of slavery in the United States by means of the thirteenth amendment to the U.S. constitution. It was passed in 1865, but resistance to slavery had been growing for not just decades, but centuries.[54] Another example is that the beginning of the end of the sacrificial cult can be traced to its centralization to Jerusalem seven or eight centuries before the fall of the Second Temple. If there had existed other Jewish temples, the sacrificial cult may have continued past 70 CE, but at that time there was only one temple, and when it was destroyed, the practice ended. Although the destruction of one single temple sufficed to finally end the sacrificial cult, the prehistory was very long indeed. Synagogue services had been in existence for a long time.

53. This is observed by, for example, Glancy, *Slavery*, 145. She describes two incorrect "trajectories, one of ascent and one of descent" in the Christian view of slavery: Either Christianity is described as completely incompatible with slavery (though it took centuries for Christians to see this, an ascent) or that ancient Christianity was an El Dorado for slaves, women, and others (and that their situation successively worsened, i.e., a descent). She argues that both models are incorrect. See, however, her more recently written book, *Slavery as Moral Problem*, 23: "The gospel Jesus proclaims is incompatible with slaveholding values." She seems to differentiate between, on the one hand, the fact that slaves and slaveholders often occur in the parables of Jesus and, on the other, the message Jesus is communicating through his teachings, which is incompatible with slavery.

54. See Harrill, *Slaves*, 165–96; Wallace, *Catholics, Slaveholders*; Avalos, *Slavery, Abolitionism*; Oshatz, *Slavery and Sin*; and, Freed, *Lincoln's Political Ambitions*.

In other words, the groundwork had been laid for a Jewish religion without the sacrificial services in the temple of Jerusalem.

A revolutionary change caused by the crucifixion would be problematic—especially if combined with a discourse of violence.[55] We must not forget that it is a story of violence, suffering, and death. The theology that is associated with the crucifixion tends therefore to be expressed in a violent way, and sometimes even assumes violent forms of expression. So often it seems there is something to "die from" or something to be "killed."[56]

There is the additional risk of describing the death of Jesus as a historical event that eliminates something that is thought to be characteristic solely of Jews or Judaism when it may not be the case, such as "pharisaism," self-righteousness, and an-eye-for-an-eye retribution (Latin *Lex talionis*). The question is if there is any part of Christian theology that expresses such sweeping judgment of Jewish faith and tradition as crucifixion theology does. One thing after another is abolished, ended, nailed up on the cross, and killed with the death of Jesus.[57] Once more—of how many times?—Jesus' *historical context* is described as his *theological contrast*. Paula Fredriksen has often noted that this stems from a desire to make the life and teaching of Jesus immediately applicable to the society of today: "Unlike Philo, or Josephus, or Hillel, or Shammai, Jesus bears the burden of being required to make immediate sense to us."[58] In short, we should avoid making statements to the effect that the teaching or death of Jesus immediately abolishes a series of concepts or behaviors. Instead, we can and should say that the cross implies a slow shift in values. The events of Good Friday and the symbol of the cross are theological points that help Christians focus on a cruciform way to think, speak, and act. The cross gives Christians a language, a renewing and uplifting language,

55. See Belousek, *Atonement*, ch. 29: "The Peace of Christ: Destroying Division, Murdering Hostility." See especially p. 542: "Through the cross, in his flesh, Jesus *puts to death*—literally, murders!—the 'hostility' that not only divides Jew from Gentile (v. 16) but disrupts relationship with God (v. 16, 18). Thus, Jesus makes peace by 'murdering hostility.'" It is surprising that he chooses the example of Jewish circumcision in this context, because the reader is then given the impression that Jewish belief in the covenant is an expression of human enmity. As so often in Christian literature, he presents Jewish life as a problem to be solved, not a way to live.

56. Saying "death is dead" expresses something else, because its source is the concept of the resurrection; see Schmemann, *For Life*, 95–106.

57. See e.g., Belousek, *Atonement*, 74, 542–49. His language becomes suddenly violent, despite his being a pacifist.

58. Fredriksen, *Jesus of Nazareth*, 268, 270.

but it would be anachronistic to apply all of our concepts and insights to the first generations of Christians. It takes time to understand what Good Friday afternoon and Easter morning mean for our views of justice, peace, freedom, restitution, forgiveness, and reconciliation.[59] In the words of Charles Caleb Colton, "the greatest friend of truth is time."

Then Choose Life!

Of the multitude of ideas, theories, and theologies about reconciliation and transformation, this book has presented two radically different ways to interpret and apply the writings on the death and resurrection of Jesus. According to one approach, the death of Jesus is a consequence, an expression, and a proof of the continued validity of the death penalty. If we are convinced that the death penalty is not a punishment but is instead a crime, can it be anything but impossible to argue that "Jesus *had* to die"? Does the conviction that "Jesus had to die" make the death penalty a nonnegotiable part of Christian reasoning? Some people are led to preach the suffering of Jesus such that they, consciously or not, accept and sanction violence as a necessary requirement for improved relations between God and humanity, and thereby among human beings. A cross theology that isolates the cross from other parts of Christian ministry risks being backward-looking and self-centered to a considerably greater degree, something theologians call becoming *incurvatus in se* (turned inward on oneself).

The second approach has been fostered and valued primarily in Eastern Christian tradition. In this approach, *anastasis* is a central pillar. The resurrection of Jesus is seen as life's victory over death—the complete opposite of death's victory over life. The transformation theology expressed in the theology of *theōsis* is so much more about accepting than it is about avoiding.[60] To die from sin, guilt, and shame is less important than to rise and live in Christ. A theology of *theōsis* can free humanity.

In Christian belief and tradition are, then, two different approaches to Good Friday and Easter. One approach emphasizes the logical necessity of death, and the other life's defiant triumph. We have to make a choice.

59. See, for example, how Belousek describes the death of Jesus as abolishing the death penalty, *Atonement*, 490–91.

60. Cf. Guroian, *Melody*, 53: "Salvation is not simply a forensic transaction that changes our *legal status* before God, but also a transformation of our *very being* that imparts to humankind a share in God's own Triune life."

> I call heaven and earth to witness against you today that I have set before you life and death, blessings and curses. Choose life so that you and your descendants may live.[61]

Holy Saturday Faith

Let us, one last time in this book, return to Holy Week. What do the days of Holy Week represent? How are they celebrated? What do they mean? Holy Thursday, the day of the institution of the Eucharist, is for many Christians the most important Communion service of the year. It might even include a ceremonial washing of feet or a ceremonial clearing the altar. The message of Easter is the joy of experiencing that humiliating defeat can be turned to victory. The disciples believed Good Friday was the end of everything, but it turned out to be the beginning of something new.

But the question now is, what does *Holy Saturday*, represent, the Saturday between Good Friday and Easter? There are no hymns in the Swedish hymnal about this day. It is not a day we celebrate in our tradition.[62] It is a day characterized by waiting. How do we do it? How is Christian faith expressed on Holy Saturday? Are there insights and beliefs we can relate to this day? In short, what can Holy Saturday mean?

Holy Saturday is about finding oneself between Good Friday afternoon and early Easter morning. The day devoted solely to the suffering and death of Jesus has passed. Observing Good Friday means dwelling upon suffering and death. It is a search for meaning in what is most difficult. Observing Holy Saturday neither denies nor debases this, but it dares to look ahead, to Easter. At the same time, there is an awareness that the absolute victory of Easter belongs to a new, unknown tomorrow. Holy Saturday mistrusts a belief that claims the battle is over and all victories won. Holy Saturday is about living in the here and now and not letting absolutely everything be defined by

61. Deut 30:19. Cf. Lossky, *Mystical Theology*, 153. Cf. Thunberg's distinction between "God's triumph as our humiliation" and "God's triumph is our triumph"; see *Den gudomliga ekonomin*, 222.

62. It is a liturgically important day in other Christian traditions. See Lindberg, "Några drag," 13. Holy Saturday is an important day in Jerusalem. It is the day the Holy Fire is lit in the Church of the Holy Sepulchre. For further viewpoints on Holy Saturday, see Svartvik, "Påskaftonstro," *Påskboken*, 112–14. The concept of Jesus descending into the underworld and preaching to the dead on the day between Good Friday and Easter morning is not being discussed here.

misfortune, suffering, and death. Yet it maintains faith without claiming that the future, with all its promises, is already here.

The death of Jesus on the afternoon of Good Friday was not the end. God would intervene and turn death into resurrection, and defeat into victory. That is why Christians still wait for the day that God is making everything new. Until then we live, in the words of a Swedish poet, in a "time of waiting" and a "time of longing."[63] Until then, the Christian faith is a Holy Saturday faith.

63. Karlfeldt, "Intet är som väntanstider," *Samlade dikter*, 161. See also Acts 17:28.

Bibliography

Anderson, Benedict. *Imagined Communities: Reflections on the Origin and Spread of Nationalism*. Rev. ed. London: Verso, 1991.

Anderson, Gary A. "Sacrifice." In *Eerdmans Dictionary of the Bible*, edited by David Noel Freedman et al., 1148–50. Grand Rapids: Eerdmans, 2000.

Anon., https://www.youtube.com/watch?v=SU1mSKuwNNo (accessed September 23, 2010).

The Apostolic Fathers. 2 vols. Edited and translated by Kirsopp Lake. London: Heinemann, 1912–13.

Athanasius of Alexandria. *Contra Gentes* and *De Incarnatione*. Edited by Robert W. Thomson. Oxford: Clarendon Press, 1971.

Aulén, Gustaf. *Christus Victor: An Historical Study of the Three Main Types of the Idea of Atonement*. London: SPCK, 1936 [in Swedish in 1930].

Aus, Roger David. *Samuel, Saul and Jesus: Three Early Palestinian Jewish Christian Gospel Haggadoth*. Atlanta: Scholars, 1994.

Avalos, Hector. *Slavery, Abolitionism, and the Ethics of Biblical Scholarship*. Sheffield, UK: Sheffield Phoenix, 2011.

Avigad, Nahman. "A Depository of Inscribed Ossuaries in the Kidron Valley." In *Israel Exploration Journal* 12.1 (1962) 1–12.

Avot de-Rabbi Natan . . . Edited by Solomon Schechter; Wien: [no publisher], [1887].

Baeck, Leo. *Harnacks Vorlesungen über das Wesen des Christentums. Sonderabdruck aus der "Monatsschrift für Geschichte u. Wissenschaft des Judentums."* 2nd ed. Breslau: Koebner, 1902.

Baker-Fletcher, Karen. *The Passion of the Lord: African American Reflections*. Edited by James A. Noel, and Matthew V. Johnson, 111–44. Minneapolis: Fortress, 2005.

Barr, James. *Fundamentalism*. 2nd ed. London: Mesorah, 1981.

Barth, Karl. *Church Dogmatics*. Edited by Geoffrey William Bromiley et al.; translation by Geoffrey William Bromiley et al. Edinburgh: T. & T. Clark, 1957–89 [in German in 1932–67].

Basler, Roy P., ed. *The Collected Works of Abraham Lincoln. Volume 8*. New Brunswick, NJ: Rutgers University Press, 1953.

Belousek, Darrin W. Snyder. *Atonement, Justice, and Peace: The Message of the Cross and the Mission of the Church*. Grand Rapids: Eerdmans, 2012.

Bengtsson, Frans G. *Sällskap för en eremit*. Stockholm: Norstedts, 1952.

Benktson, Benkt Erik. *Samtidighetens mirakel: Kring tidsproblematiken i Lars Gyllenstens romaner*. Stockholm: Bonniers, 1989.

Bentzer, Tage. *Lagen och nåden: Ett studium av Galaterbrevet* . . . 4th ed. Arlöv, Sweden: Skeab, 1982.

Bergman, Martin. *Dödsstraffet, kyrkan och staten i Sverige från 1700-tal till 1900-tal.* Stockholm: Nerenius & Santérus, 1996.

———. "Fighting the Death Penalty with Theological Arguments: Tactics and Faith among 19th Century Abolitionists." *Kyrkohistorisk årsskrift* 107 (2007) 71–89.

Berkowitz, Beth A. *Execution and Invention: Death Penalty Discourse in Early Rabbinic and Christian Cultures.* Oxford: Oxford University Press, 2006.

Best, Ernest. *A Critical and Exegetical Commentary on Ephesians.* Edinburgh: T. & T. Clark, 1998.

de Béthune, Pierre-François. *Interreligious Hospitality: The Fulfillment of Dialogue.* Translated by Robert Henrey; Collegeville, MN: Liturgical, 2010 [in French in 2007].

Bialik, Haim Nahman. *Halachah and Aggadah.* Translated by Julius I. Segal; London: Education Department of the Zionist Federation of Great Britain and Ireland, 1944 [in Hebrew in 1916].

———. "Law and Legend." In *The Canadian Jewish Chronicle*, March 28, 1945, 35–42.

Bibeln, med noter, parallellhänvisningar och uppslagsdel samt hittlistan—en liten hjälp att upptäcka Bibeln. Stockholm: Cordia, 2001 [= Bible 2000; in Swedish: Bibel 2000].

Bibeln eller den heliga skrift. Gamla och Nya testamentet. De kanoniska böckerna. Översättningen gillad och stadfäst av konungen den 2 oktober 1917 . . . Stockholm: Evangeliska Fosterlands-Stiftelsens förlags-expedition, 1920 [translated in 1917].

Biblia Hebraica Stuttgartensia . . . *Editio secunda emandata* . . . Edited by W. Rudolph, and H. P. Rüger. Stuttgart: Deutsche Bibelgesellschaft, 1984.

Borg, Marcus J. *Conflict, Holiness, and Politics in the Teaching of Jesus.* 2nd ed. Harrisburg: Trinity Press International, 1998.

Boyarin, Daniel. *Dying for God: Martyrdom and the Making of Christianity and Judaism.* Stanford: Stanford University Press, 1999.

———. *The Jewish Gospels: The Story of the Jewish Christ.* New York: New, 2012.

Boys, Mary C. *Redeeming our Sacred Story: The Death of Jesus and Relations between Jews and Christians.* Mahwah, NJ: Paulist, 2013.

Branham, Joan R. "Penetrating the Sacred: Breaches and Barriers in the Jerusalem Temple." In *Thresholds of the Sacred: Architectural, Art Historical, Liturgical, and Theological Perspectives on Religious Screens, East and West*, edited by Sharon Gerstel, 6–24. Cambridge: Harvard University Press, 2006.

Brock, Rita Nakashima, and Rebecca Ann Parker. *Proverbs of Ashes: Violence, Redemptive Suffering, and the Search for What Saves Us.* Boston: Beacon, 2001.

Brock, Rita Nakashima. "The Cross of Resurrection and Communal Redemption." In *Cross-Examinations: Readings on the Meaning of the Cross Today*, edited by Marit Trelstad, 241–51. Minneapolis: Fortress, 2006.

Brodd, Sven-Erik, and Alf Härdelin, eds. *Maria i Sverige under tusen år: Föredrag vid symposiet i Vadstena 6–10 oktober 1994.* 2 vols. Skellefteå, Sweden: Artos, 1996.

Brown, Raymond E. *The Death of the Messiah: From Gethsemane to the Grave.* 2 vols. New York: Doubleday, 1994.

Bullard, F. Lauriston. *Abraham Lincoln & the Widow Bixby.* New Brunswick, NJ: Rutgers University Press, 1946.

Buren, Paul M. van. *A Theology of the Jewish-Christian Reality.* 3 vols. San Francisco: Harper & Row, 1980–88.

Camnerin, Sofia, and Arne Fritzon. *Försoning behövs.* Stockholm: Verbum, 2012.

Carroll, James. *Constantine's Sword: The Church and the Jews. A History*. Boston: Houton Miflin, 2001.

Castelli, Elizabeth A. *Martyrdom and Memory: Early Christian Culture Making*. New York: Columbia University Press, 2004.

Catalano, Rosann M. "A Matter of Perspective: An Alternative Reading of Mark 15:38." In *Seeing Judaism Anew: Christianity's Sacred Obligation*, edited by Mary C. Boys, 187–99. Lanham, MD: Rowman & Littlefield, 2005.

Catholic Encyclopedia. Edited by Charles George Herbermann. New York: Encyclopedia, 1907–14.

Cavanaugh, William T. *Torture and Eucharist: Theology, Politics, and the Body of Christ*. Oxford: Wiley-Blackwell, 1998.

Chapman, David W. *Ancient Jewish and Christian Perceptions of Crucifixion*. Grand Rapids: Baker Academic, 2010.

Cheney, Michael. *Dust, Wind and Agony: Character, Speech and Genre in Job*. Stockholm: Almqvist & Wiksell International, 1994.

Claman, Henry N. *Jewish Images in the Christian Church: Art as the Mirror of the Jewish-Christian Conflict 200–1250 C.E.* Macon, GA: Mercer University Press, 2000.

Clément, Olivier. "Introduktion till den ortodoxa kyrkans liv och lära." In *Ortodox spiritualitet*, edited by Gunborg Blomstrand, 23–38. Uppsala: KISA, 1989.

Cobb, John B., ed. *Christian Faith and Religious Diversity: Mobilization for the Human Family*. Minneapolis: Fortress, 2002.

Cohen, Jeremy. *Christ Killers: The Jews and the Passion from the Bible to the Big Screen*. Oxford: Oxford University Press, 2007.

Cohen, Raymond. *Negotiating across Cultures: International Communication in an Interdependent World*. 2nd ed. Washington, DC: United States Institute of Peace, 1997.

Cohick, Lynn. "Melito of Sardis's PERI PASCHA and Its 'Israel.'" *Harvard Theological Review* 91.4 (1998) 351–72.

Collins, Paul M. *Partaking in Divine Nature*. London: T. & T. Clark, 2010.

Cone, James H. *The Cross and the Lynching Tree*. Maryknoll, NY: Orbis, 2011.

Corley, Kathleen E., and Robert L. Webb, eds. *Jesus and Mel Gibson's the Passion of the Christ: The Film, the Gospels and the Claims of History*. New York: Continuum, 2004.

Cranfield, C. E. B. *A Critical and Exegetical Commentary on the Epistle to the Romans*. 2 vols. Edinburgh: T. & T. Clark, 1975–79.

Crossan, John Dominic. "Hymn to a Savage God." In *Jesus and Mel Gibson's the Passion of the Christ: The Film, the Gospels and the Claims of History*, edited by Kathleen E. Corley and Robert L. Webb, 8–27. New York: Continuum, 2004.

———. "What Victory? What God? A Review Debate with N. T. Wright on *Jesus and the Victory of God*." *Scottish Journal of Theology* 50.3 (1997) 345–58.

Cunneen, Sally. *In Search of Mary: The Woman and the Symbol*. New York: Ballantine, 1996.

Cunningham, Philip C., ed. *Pondering the Passion: What's at Stake for Christians and Jews?* Lanham, MD: Rowman & Littlefield, 2004.

Cyril of Jerusalem. *Catechetical Lectures*. https://www.crossroadsinitiative.com/media/articles/jerusalem-catecheses-12-24-cyril-of-jerusalem (accessed September 29, 2017).

Daube, David. *The New Testament and Rabbinic Judaism*. 1956. Reprint, Peabody, MA: Hendrickson, 1990.

Davies, W. D., and Dale C. Allison. *The Gospel according to Saint Matthew*. 3 vols. Edinburgh: T. & T. Clark, 1988–97.

De apostoliska fäderna: Inledning, översättning och förklaringar av Olof Andrén och Per Beskow. Stockholm: Verbum, 1992.

Den svenska kyrkohandboken. Del I . . . Stockholm: Verbum, 1987.

Den svenska kyrkohandboken: Stadfäst av Konungen år 1942. Stockholm: Svenska kyrkans diakonistyrelses bokförlag, 1942.

Den svenska psalmboken med tillägg. Stockholm: Verbum, 2002.

Dibelius, Martin. *James: A Commentary on the Epistle of James*. Revised by Heinrich Greeven; translated by Michael A. Williams; edited by Helmut Koester. Philadelphia: Fortress, 1975 [in German in 1964].

Dorff, Elliot N. *The Way Into* Tikkun Olam *(Repairing the World)*. Woodstock, VT: Jewish Lights, 2005.

Dunn, James D. G. "The New Perspective on Paul." *Bulletin of the John Rylands Library* 65 (1983) 94–122.

Eastman, Susan Grove. "Israel and the Mercy of God: A Re-reading of Galatians 6.16 and Romans 9–11." *New Testament Studies* 56 (2010) 367–95.

Eisenbaum, Pamela. *Paul Was Not a Christian: The Original Message of a Misunderstood Apostle*. New York: HarperOne, 2009.

Elazar, Daniel J. "How Religious Are Israeli Jews?" https://www.jcpa.org/dje/articles2/howrelisr.htm (accessed January 8, 2013).

Eliot, T. S. *Four Quartets*. London: Faber & Faber, 1949.

Eskenazi, Tamara Cohn. "Introduction—Facing the Text as Other: Some Implications of Levinas's Work for Biblical Studies." In *Levinas and Biblical Studies*, edited by Tamara Cohn Eskenazi et al., 1–16. Atlanta: Society of Biblical Literature, 2003.

———. "With the Song of Songs in Our Hearts." In *Chapters of the Heart: Jewish Women Sharing the Torah of Our Lives*, 176–85. Eugene, OR: Cascade, 2013.

Eskenazi, Tamara Cohn, et al., eds. *The Sabbath in Jewish and Christian Traditions*. New York: Crossroad, 1991.

Feder, Yitzhaq. *Blood Expiation in Hittite and Biblical Ritual: Origins, Context, and Meaning*. Atlanta: Society of Biblical Literature, 2011.

Finlan, Stephen, and Vladimir Kharlamov. *Theōsis: Deification in Christian Theology*. Eugene, OR: Pickwick, 2006.

Fiorenza, Elisabeth Schüssler. "The Cross as a Central Christian Symbol of Injustice." *Tikkun* 27.4 (2012) 30–32.

Flannery, Edward H. *The Anguish of the Jews: Twenty-Three Centuries of Antisemitism. Revised and Updated*. Mahwah, NJ: Paulist, 1995.

Ford, David F. *Self and Salvation: Being Transformed*. Cambridge: Cambridge University Press, 1999.

Forster, Edward Morgan. *Aspects of the Novel*. Edited by Oliver Stallybrass. London: Penguin, 1990.

Foster, Paul. "The Epistle to Diognetus." *Expository Times* 118.4 (2007) 162–68.

Franklin, John Hope, and Alfred Am Moss Jr. *From Slavery to Freedom: A History of African Americans*. Boston: McGraw-Hill, 8th ed. 2000.

Franklin, Robert M. "The Passion and African American Pilgrimage." In *The Passion of the Lord: African American Reflections*, edited by James A. Noel, and Matthew V. Johnson, 160–74. Minneapolis: Fortress, 2005.

Fredriksen, Paula. "Did Jesus Oppose the Purity Laws?" *Bible Review* 11.3 (1995) 18–25 and 42–47.

———. "*Excaecati occulta justitia Dei*: Augustine on Jews and Judaism." *Journal of Early Christian Studies* 3.3 (1995) 299–324.

———. *From Jesus to Christ: The Origins of the New Testament Images of Jesus*. New Haven, CT: Yale University Press, 1988.

———. *Jesus of Nazareth: King of the Jews: A Jewish Life and the Emerge of Christianity*. New York: Knopf, 1999.

———, ed. *On the Passion of the Christ: Exploring the Issues Raised by the Controversial Movie*. Berkeley: University of California Press, 2006. [Previously published under the title *Perspectives on the Passion of the Christ: Religious Thinkers and Writers Explore the Issues Raised by the Controversial Movie*, edited by Paula Fredriksen. New York: Miramax, 2004.]

———. *Sin: The Early History of an Idea*. Princeton: Princeton University Press, 2012.

———. "Yom Kippur: WWJD?" *Huffington Post*, September 25, 2012. https://www.huffingtonpost.com/paula-fredriksen/yom-kippur-what-would-jesus-do_b_1910759.html (accessed December 28, 2013).

Fredriksen, Paula, and Jesper Svartvik, eds. *Krister among the Jews and Gentiles: Essays in Appreciation of the Life and Work of Krister Stendahl*. Mahwah, NJ: Paulist, 2018.

Freed, Edwin D. *Lincoln's Political Ambitions, Slavery, and the Bible*. Eugene, OR: Pickwick, 2012.

Frid, Bo, and Jesper Svartvik. *Thomasevangeliet med Jesusorden från Oxyrhynchus (P. Oxy. 1, 654, 655)* . . . 2nd ed. Lund: Arcus, 2004.

Fridrichsen, Anton. *Fyrahanda sädesåker: En kommentar till Evangeliebokens högmässotexter*. Edited by Birger Gerhardsson. Stockholm: Svenska kyrkans diakonistyrelses bokförlag, 1958.

Garrett, Greg. *Stories from the Edge: A Theology of Grief*. Louisville, KY: Westminster John Knox, 2008.

Gaston, Lloyd. "The Uniqueness of Jesus as a Methodological Problem." In *Origins and Method: Towards a New Understanding of Judaism and Christianity. Essays in Honour of John C. Hurd*, edited by Bradley H. McLean, 271–81. Sheffield, UK: Sheffield Academic, 1993.

Gilbert, Martin. *Kristallnacht: Prelude to Destruction*. New York: HarperCollins, 2006.

Gillman, Neil. *Believing and Its Tensions: A Personal Conversation about God, Torah, Suffering and Death in Jewish Thought*. Woodstock, VT: Jewish Lights, 2013.

Girard, René. *Violence and the Sacred*. Translated by Patrick Gregory. Baltimore: Johns Hopkins University Press, 1977 [in French in 1972].

Glancy, Jennifer A. *Slavery as Moral Problem: In the Early Church and Today*. Minneapolis: Fortress, 2011.

———. *Slavery in Early Christianity*. Oxford: Oxford University Press, 2002.

Goodhart, Sandor, and Ann W. Astell. "Substitutive Reading: An Introduction to Girardian Thinking, Its Reception in Biblical Studies, and This Volume." In *Sacrifice, Scripture, and Substitution: Readings in Ancient Judaism and Christianity*, edited by Ann W. Astell, and Sandor Goodhart, 1–36. Notre Dame, IN: University of Notre Dame Press, 2011.

Gordon, Ph[ilippus]. *Judarnas högtider i hemmet och synagogan*. Stockholm: Israelsmissionens bokförlag, 1910.

Gorman, Michael J. *Inhabiting the Cruciform God: Kenosis, Justification, and Theosis in Paul's Narrative Soteriology*. Grand Rapids: Eerdmans, 2009.

Grantén, Eva-Lotta. *Utanför paradiset: Arvsyndsläran i nutida luthersk teologi och etik*. Stockholm: Verbum, 2013.

Greenstein, Edward L. "The Invention of Language in the Poetry of Job." In *Interested Readers: Essays on the Hebrew Bible in Honor of David J. A. Clines*, edited by James K. Aitken et al., 331–46. Atlanta: Society of Biblical Literature, 2013.

———. "Truth or Theodicy? Speaking Truth to Power in the Book of Job." *The Princeton Seminary Bulletin* 27 (2006) 238–58.

Gritsch, Erik W. *Martin Luther's Anti-Semitism: Against His Better Judgment*. Grand Rapids: Eerdmans, 2012.

"Guds vägar." *Svensk Teologisk Kvartalskrift* 79.3 (2003) 114–21.

Gunton, Colin E. *The Actuality of Atonement: A Study of Metaphor, Rationality and the Christian Tradition*. Edinburgh: T. & T. Clark, 1988.

Guroian, Vigen, *The Melody of Faith: Theology in an Orthodox Key*. Grand Rapids: Eerdmans, 2010.

Gurtner, Daniel M. *The Torn Veil: Matthew's Exposition of the Death of Jesus*. Cambridge: Cambridge University Press, 2007.

Hagner, Donald A. *Matthew*. 2 vols. Dallas: Word, 1993–95.

Halbertal, Moshe. *On Sacrifice*. Princeton: Princeton University Press, 2012.

Halldorf, Peter. "Symeon: teologi i Ande och sanning." In *Ljusets källa: Trettio andliga hymner av Symeon den nye teologen*, translated by Olof Andrén, 7–20. Skellefteå, Sweden: Artos, 2006.

Harrill, J. Albert. *Slaves in the New Testament: Literary, Social, and Moral Dimensions*. Minneapolis: Fortress, 2006.

Hedqvist, Vilhelm. *Petrus evangelium, Petrus uppenbarelse och de tolf apostlarnes lära. Öfversättning med förklarande anmärkningar*. Stockholm: Palmquist, 1893.

Heim, S. Mark. "Saved by What Shouldn't Happen: The Anti-Sacrificial Meaning of the Cross." In *Cross-Examinations: Readings on the Meaning of the Cross Today*, edited by Marit Trelstad, 211–24. Minneapolis: Fortress, 2006.

———. *Saved from Sacrifice: A Theology of the Cross*. Grand Rapids: Eerdmans, 2006.

Hengel, Martin. *Crucifixion the Ancient World and the Folly of the Cross*. Translated by John Bowden. London: SCM, 1977 [in German in 1976].

Heschel, Abraham Joshua. *God in Search of Man: A Philosophy of Judaism*. New York: Farrar, Straus & Giroux, 1955.

———. *Heavenly Torah as Refracted through the Generations*. Edited and translated by Gordon Tucker et al. New York: Continuum, 2005 [in Hebrew in 1962–95].

———. *The Sabbath: Its Meaning for Modern Man*. New York: Farrar, Straus & Giroux, 1951.

———. "Untitled" (In Yiddish *On a nomen*). In *The Ineffable Name of God: Man. Poems. Translated from the Yiddish by Morton M. Leifman. Introduction by Edward K. Kaplan*. New York: Continuum, 2004 [in Yiddish in 1933].

Heschel, Susannah. *The Aryan Jesus: Christian Theologians and the Bible in Nazi Germany*. Princeton: Princeton University Press, 2008.

Hoffman, Lawrence A. "Jewish and Christian Liturgy." In *Christianity in Jewish Terms*, edited by Tikva Frymer-Kensky et al., 175–89. Boulder, CO: Westview, 2000.

Holmquist, Harriet. *Mötesplats Jerusalem*. Göteborg: Gothia, 1985.

Irving, Edward. *The Collected Writings of Edward Irving in Five Volumes*. 5 vols. Edited by Gavin Carlyle. London: Alexander Strahan, 1864–65.

Iustini Martyris Dialogus Cum Tryphone. Edited by Miroslav Marcovich. Berlin: de Gruyter, 1997.

Jakubowski, Jackie. *Ljudet av alef: Judiska tankar om hemmahörande, minne, identitet, Gud och diasporan*. Stockholm: Natur & Kultur, 2000.

Johnson, Matthew V. "Lord of the Crucified." In *The Passion of the Lord: African American Reflections*, edited by James A. Noel, and Matthew V. Johnson, 1–32. Minneapolis: Fortress, 2005.

Josephus in Ten Volumes. 10 vols. Translated by H. St. J. Thackerey et al. Cambridge: Harvard University Press, 1926–65.

Jospe, Raphael. "Pluralism out of the Sources of Judaism: The Quest for Religious Pluralism without Relativism." In *Jewish Theology and World Religions*, edited by Alon Goshen-Gottstein and Eugene Korn, 87–121 . Oxford: Littman Library of Jewish Civilization, 2012.

Judiska ordspråk: Sammanställda och översatta av Lennart Kerbel. 2nd ed. Stockholm: Megilla-Förlaget, 2009.

Kaminsky, Joel S. *Yet I Loved Jacob: Reclaiming the Biblical Concept of Election*. Nashville, TN: Abingdon, 2007.

Karlfeldt, Erik Axel. *Samlade dikter: Med kommentarer av Johan Stenström*. Stockholm: Wahlström & Widstrand, 2001.

Keckley, Elizabeth. *Behind the Scenes in the Lincoln White House: Memoirs of an African-American Seamstress*. Mineola: Dover, 2006. [Originally published in 1868 under the title *Behind the Scenes: Or, Thirty Years a Slave, and Four Years in the White House*.]

Kelly, William. *Lectures on the Gospel of Matthew*. London: Morrish, 1868.

Kessler, Herbert L., and David Nirenberg, eds. *Judaism and Christian Art: Aesthetic Anxieties from the Catacombs to Colonialism*. Philadelphia: University of Pennsylvania Press, 2011.

Kharlamov, Vladimir. *Theōsis: Deification in Christian Theology. Volume* 2. Eugene, OR: Pickwick, 2011.

Kieffer, René. *Johannesevangeliet 1–10*. Uppsala: EFS-förlaget, 1987.

Kitchen, Martin. *Ephesians*. London: Routledge, 1994.

Klein, Isaac. *A Guide to Jewish Religious Practice. A Supplement by Rabbi Joel Roth*. New York: Jewish Theological Seminary of America, 1992.

Klijn, A. F. J. "2 (Syriac Apocalypse of) Baruch: A New Translation and Introduction." In *The Old Testament Pseudepigrapha. Volume 1: Apocalyptic Literature and Testaments*, edited by James H. Charlesworth, 615–20. New York: Doubleday, 1983.

Käsemann, Ernst. *New Testament Questions of Today*. Translated by W. J. Montague. Philadelphia: Fortress, 1979 [in German in 1965].

Larsson, Edvin. *Apostlagärningarna 13–20*. Uppsala: EFS-förlaget, 1987.

Larsson, Göran. *Fönster mot Gud: Ikonernas budskap i Svenska teologiska institutets kapell i Jerusalem*. Lund: Arcus, 2011.

———. *Tid för Gud: Judiska och kristna perspektiv på de judiska högtiderna*. Lund: Arcus, 2006.

Levine, Baruch A. *The JPS Torah Commentary: Leviticus*. Philadelphia: Jewish Publication Society, 1989.

Levine, Lee I. *The Ancient Synagogue: The First Thousand Years*. 2nd ed. New Haven, CT: Yale University Press, 2005.

Lied, Liv Ingeborg. "Those Who Know and Those Who Don't: Mystery, Instruction, and Knowledge in 2 *Baruch*." In *Mystery and Secrecy in the Nag Hammadi Collection and Other Ancient Literature: Ideas and Practices*, edited by Christian H. Bull et al., 427–46. Leiden: Brill, 2011.

Lieu, Judith. *Image & Reality: The Jews in the World of the Christians in the Second Century*. Edinburgh: T. & T. Clark, 1996.

Lincoln, Andrew T. *Ephesians*. Nashville, TN: Thomas Nelson, 1990.

Lindberg, Annicka. "Några drag i den ortodoxa kyrkans liv." In *Ortodox spiritualitet*, edited by Gunborg Blomstrand, 7–21. Uppsala: KISA, 1989.

Lindblom, Johannes. *Boken om Job och hans lidande*. Lund: Gleerups, 1940.

Ljungman, Henrik. *Guds barmhärtighet och dom: Fariséernas lära om de två "måtten."* Lund: Gleerup, 1950.

Lossky, Vladimir. *The Mystical Theology of the Eastern Church*. Crestwood, NY: St. Vladimir's Seminary, 1976 [in French in 1944].

Lundborg, Matheus. *Det s. k. Petrusevangeliet, ett nyfunnet fragment ur en fornkristlig apokryf. Text med öfversättning och kritisk undersökning*. Lund: Gleerups, 1893.

Luther, Martin. *Martin Luther's Basic Theological Writings. Foreword by Jaroslav Pelikan*. Edited by Timothy F. Lull and William R. Russell. 2nd ed. Minneapolis: Fortress, 2005.

Lycke, Erik. *Flavius Josephus: Mer romare än jude*. Stockholm: Atlantis, 1999.

Mahlmann, Theodor. "Die Rechtfertigung ist der Artikel, mit dem die Kirche steht und fällt." In *Zur Rechtfertigungslehre in der Lutherischen Orthodoxie*, edited by Udo Sträter, 167–271 . Leipzig: Evangelische Verlagsanstalt, 2003.

Mantzaridis, Georgios I. *The Deification of Man: St Gregory Palamas and the Orthodox Tradition, with a Foreword by Bishop Kallistos Ware of Diokleia*. Translated by Liadain Sherrard. New York: St. Vladimir's Seminary, 1984 [in Greek in 1963].

Marrou, Henri Irenée. *Au Diognète: Introduction, édition critique, traduction et commentaire*. Paris: Cerf, 1951.

Martola, Nils. *Kommentar till påskhaggadan*. Åbo: Åbo akademi, 1988.

Marty, Martin E., and R. Scott Appleby. *Fundamentalisms Comprehended*. Chicago: University of Chicago Press, 1995.

Mauss, Marcel. *The Gift: The Form and Reason for Exchange in Archaic Society: With a Foreword by Mary Douglas*. London: Routledge, 1990 [in French in 1950].

McKnight, Scot. *The Real Mary: Why Evangelical Christians Can Embrace the Mother of Jesus*. Brewster, MA: Paraclete, 2007.

Meecham, Henry G. *The Epistle to Diognetus: The Greek Text*. Manchester, UK: Manchester University Press, 1949.

Mekilta De-Rabbi Ishmael. 3 vols. Edited by Jacob Z. Lauterbach. Philadelphia: Jewish Publication Society, 1933.

Melito av Sardes. *Om påsken. Översatt från grekiskan och kommenterad av Per Beskow*. Skellefteå, Sweden: Artos, 1984.

Melito of Sardis. *On Pascha and Fragments*. Edited by Stuart George Hall. Oxford: Clarendon, 1979.

Midrash rabbah: 'Im kol ha-mepharshim. Jerusalem: Wagshal, [no year].

Milgrom, Jacob. *Cult and Conscience: The Asham and the Priestly Doctrine of Repentance*. Leiden: Brill, 1976.

———. *The JPS Torah Commentary: Numbers*. Philadelphia: Jewish Publication Society, 1990.

———. *Leviticus 1–16: A New Translation with Introduction and Commentary*. New York: Doubleday, 1991.

———. *Leviticus: A Book of Ritual and Ethics. A Continental Commentary*. Minneapolis: Fortress, 2004.

Millgram, Abraham E. *Jewish Worship*. Philadelphia: Jewish Publication Society, 1971.

Mishnayoth . . . 7 vols. Edited by Philip Blackman. 2nd ed. Gateshead, UK: Judaica, 1983.

Mitton, C. Leslie. *The Epistle to the Ephesians: Its Authorship, Origin and Purpose*. Oxford: Clarendon, 1951.

Modéus, Martin. *Sacrifice and Symbol: Biblical Šĕlamîm in a Ritual Perspective*. Stockholm: Almqvist & Wiksell International, 2005.

Montefiore, Claude G. *The Synoptic Gospels: Edited with an Introduction and a Commentary*. 2 vols. 2nd ed. London: Macmillan, 1927.

Moss, Candida. *The Myth of Persecution: How Early Christians Invented a Story of Martyrdom*. San Francisco: HarperOne, 2013.

Moyaert, Marianne. *Fragile Identities: Towards a Theology of Interreligious Hospitality*. Amsterdam: Rodopi, 2011.

Myers, Benjamin. *Christ the Stranger: The Theology of Rowan Williams*. London: T. & T. Clark, 2012.

Nag Hammadi Codex II, 2–7 Together with XIII,2 Brit. Lib. Or.4926(1) and P.Oxy. 1, 654, 655 . . . Vol. I. Gospel according to Thomas*. Edited by B. Layton. Leiden: Brill, 1989.

Nellas, Panayiotis. *Deification in Christ: Orthodox Persepctives on the Nature of the Human Person*. With a Foreword by Bishop Kallistos Ware of Diokleia. Translated by Norman Russell. New York: St. Vladimir's Seminary, 1987 [in Greek in 1979].

Niebuhr, H. Richard. *The Meaning of Revelation*. Introduction by Douglas F. Ottati. Louisville: Westminster John Knox, 2006.

Niebuhr, Reinhold, *The Nature and Destiny of Man: A Christian Interpretation. Introduction by Robin W. Lovin. Volume I: Human Nature & Volume II: Human Destiny*. Louisville, KY: Westminster John Knox, 1996.

Nirenberg, David. *Anti-Judaism: The Western Tradition*. New York: Norton, 2013.

Noel, James A., and Matthew V. Johnson, eds. *The Passion of the Lord: African American Reflections*. Minneapolis: Fortress, 2005.

Noel, James A. "Were You There?" In *The Passion of the Lord: African American Reflections*, edited by James A. Noel and Matthew V. Johnson, 33–50. Minneapolis: Fortress, 2005.

Novum Testamentum Graece . . . Editione vicesima septima revisa. Edited by Barbara and Kurt Aland et al. Stuttgart: Deutsche Bibelgesellschaft, 2004.

Odeberg, Hugo. "Det är fullbordat: Morgonandakt i radio måndagen den 28 mars 1955." *Svenska Morgonbladet*, March 29, 1955.

Oshatz, Molly. *Slavery and Sin: The Fight against Slavery and the Rise of Liberal Protestantism*. Oxford: Oxford University Press, 2012.

The Oxyrhynchus Papyri. Part III. Edited by Bernard P. Grenfell and Arthur S. Hunt. London: Egypt Exploration Fund, 1903.

Ozarowski, Joseph. "*Keri'ah*: The Tearing of the Garment." In *Jewish Insights on Death and Mourning*, edited by Jack Riemer; preface by Sherwin B. Nuland. New York: Schocken, 1995. [Originally published under the title *Wrestling with the Angel*.]

Parkes, James. "A Reappraisal of the Christian Attitude to Judaism." *Journal of Bible and Religion* 29.4 (1961) 299–307.

Patrologiae cursus completus: Series graeca. 162 vols. Edited by Jacques Paul Migne. Paris, 1857–66.

Patrologiae cursus completus: Series latina. 221 vols. Edited by Jacques Paul Migne. Paris, 1844–64.

Patton, Kimberley C. "Foreword." In Albert J. Raboteau, *A Sorrowful Joy: The Harold M. Wit Lectures . . .*, 1–9. Mahwah, NJ: Paulist, 2002.

Pawlikowski, John T. *Pope John Paul II on Christian-Jewish Relations: His Legacy, Our Challenges*. The Inaugural Annual John Paul II Lecture on Christian Jewish Relations. Boston: Boston College [Center for Christian-Jewish Learning], 2012.

Pelc, Julie [Adler]. "'Talk to Me': Wisdom from the Book of Job 42 (When *More* Bad Things Happen to Good People)." Unpublished article, written at Hebrew Union College, Los Angeles, 2006.

Pelikan, Jaroslav. *Jesus through the Centuries: His Place in the History of Culture*. New York: Harper & Row, 1987.

———. *Mary through the Centuries: Her Place in the History of Culture*. New Haven, CT: Yale University Press, 1996.

Perler, Othmar. "L'Evangile de Pierre et Méliton de Sardis." *Revue Biblique* 71 (1964) 584–90.

Perrin, Nicholas. *Jesus the Temple*. Grand Rapids: Baker Academic, 2010.

Pesikta de-Rab Kahana . . . Translated by William G. [Gershon Zev] Braude, and Israel J. Kapstein. London: Routledge & Kegan Paul, 1975.

Pesiqta de-Rav Kahana . . . 2 vols. New York: Beit ha-midrash le-rabbanim shebe-Ameriqah, [1987].

Philo in Ten Volumes . . . . Translated by F. H. Colson, and G. H. Whitaker. Cambridge: Harvard University Press, 1934.

Piltz, Anders. *Som regnet och snön: Ett kyrkoår*. Skellefteå: Artos, 1995.

Pirḳē de Rabbi Eliezer . . . . Edited by Gerald Friedlander. 4th ed. New York: Sepher-Hermon, 1981.

[Sepher] Pirqe Rabbi Eli'ezer . . . Jerusalem: [no publisher], [1970].

Plantinga, Richard J., ed. *Christianity and Pluralism: Classic and Contemporary Readings*. Oxford: Blackwell, 1999.

———, et al. *An Introduction to Christian Theology*. Cambridge: Cambridge University Press, 2010.

Plate, S. Brent, ed. *Re-Viewing the Passion: Mel Gibson's Film and Its Critics*. New York: Palgrave Macmillan, 2004.

Popov, Ivan V. "The Idea of Deification in the Early Eastern Church." In *Theōsis: Deification in Christian Theology, Volume 2*, edited by Vladimir Kharlamov, 42–82. Eugene, OR: Pickwick, 2011.

Raphael, Frederic. *A Jew among Romans: The Life and Legacy of Flavius Josephus*. New York: Anchor, 2013.

Reinhartz, Adele. "'Jews' and Jews in the Fourth Gospel." In *Anti-Judaism and the Fourth Gospel*, edited by Reimund Bieringer et al., 213–27. Louisville, KY: Westminster John Knox, 2001.

Richards, Hubert J. *Death and After: What Will Really Happen?* London: Fount, 1980.

Rosen, Jonathan. *The Talmud and the Internet: A Journey between Worlds*. New York: Farrar, Straus & Giroux, 2000.

Rowe, C. Kavin. "The Hope of the Cross." *Tikkun* 27.4 (2012) 28–29.

Ruether, Rosemary R. *Introducing Redemption in Christian Feminism*. Cleveland, OH: Pilgrim, 1998.

Schmemann, Alexander. *For Life of the World: Sacraments and Orthodoxy*. 2nd ed. Crestwood, NY: St Vladimir's Seminary, 1973.

Scherman, Nossan, ed. *The Complete Artscroll Siddur*. New York: Mesorah Publications, 1984.

Schieber, Vicki, et al. *Where Justice and Mercy Meet: Catholic Opposition to the Death Penalty*. Collegeville, MN: Liturgical, 2013.

Schreiter, Robert J. *The Ministry of Reconciliation: Spirituality & Strategies*. Maryknoll, NY: Orbis, 1998.

Schrenk, Gottlob. "*biazomai*." In *Theological Dictionary of the New Testament*, 10 vols., edited by Gerhard Kittel; translated by Geoffrey William Bromiley, 1:609–13. Grand Rapids: Eerdmans, 1964–76 [in German in 1933–49].

Schürer, Emil. *The History of the Jewish People in the Age of Jesus Christ (175 B.C.–A.D. 135)*. 4 vols. Edited by Geza Vermes et al. Rev. ed. Edinburgh: T. & T. Clark, 1979.

Schäfer, Peter. *Judeophobia: Attitudes toward the Jews in the Ancient World*. Cambridge: Harvard University Press, 1997.

Septuaginta . . . Edited by Alfred Rahlfs. Stuttgart: Deutsche Bibelgesellschaft, 1979.

Seth, Ivar. *Överheten och svärdet: Dödsstraffsdebatten i Sverige 1809–1974*. Edited by Stig Jägerskiöld. Stockholm: Institutet för rättshistorisk forskning, 1984.

Siri, Edward. *Walking with Mary: A Biblical Journey from Nazareth to the Cross*. New York: Image, 2013.

Sjögren, Monika. *Det var en gång en vallareman: Boken om Göte Hedenquist: En modig präst och en ovanlig pappa*. Stockholm: Kulturhistoriska Bokförlaget, 2013.

Smith, William Robertson. *Lectures on the Religion of the Semites: The Fundamental Institutions*. New York: Macmillan, 1927.

Snoek, Jan A. M. "Defining 'Rituals.'" In *Theorizing Rituals: Classical Topics, Theoretical Approaches, Analytical Concepts*, edited by Jens Kreinath et al., 3–14. Leiden: Brill, 2008.

Sommer, Benjamin D. "Isaiah." In *The Jewish Study Bible*, edited by Adele Berlin and Marc Zvi Brettler, 780–916. Oxford: Oxford University Press, 2004.

Sources chrétiennes. Paris, Édition du Cerf, 1941–.

Stacpoole, Alberic, ed. *Mary in Doctrine and Devotion*. Dublin: Columba, 1990.

Stark, Rodney. *The Rise of Christianity: How the Obscure, Marginal Jesus Movement Became the Dominant Religious Force in the Western World in a Few Centuries*. San Francisco: Harper San Francisco, 1997.

Starr, James M. *Sharers in Divine Nature: 2 Peter 1:4 in Its Hellenistic Context*. Stockholm: Almquist & Wiksell, 2000.

Stemberger, Günther. *Introduction to the Talmud and Midrash*. Translated and edited by Markus Bockmuehl. 2nd ed. Edinburgh: T. & T. Clark, 1996.

Stendahl, Krister. *Energy for Life: Reflections on a Theme. "Come, Holy Spirit—Renew the Whole Creation."* 2nd ed. Brewster, MA: Paraclete, 1999.

———. *Final Account: Paul's Letter to the Romans*. Minneapolis: Fortress, 1995.

———. *Holy Week Preaching*. 2nd ed. Philadelphia: Fortress, 1985.

———. *Paul among Jews and Gentiles and Other Essays*. Minneapolis: Fortress, 1976.

Stevers, Dan. "The Veil." https://www.youtube.com/watch?v=UcpTiV_DzVE&feature=related (accessed December 28, 2013).

Stone, Michael E., and Matthias Henze. *4 Ezra and 2 Baruch: Translations, Introductions, and Notes*. Minneapolis: Fortress, 2013.

Svartvik, Jesper. *Bibeltolkningens bakgator: Synen på judar, slavar och homosexuella i historia och nutid*. Stockholm: Verbum, 2006.

———. "Contemporary Christian Self-Understanding: *Populus Dei* or *Corpus Christi*?" *Current Dialogue* 53 (2013) 32–38.

———. "'East Is East, and West Is West': The Concept of Torah in Paul and Mark." In *Mark and Paul: Comparative Essays. Part I: Two Authors at the Beginning of Christianity*, edited by Oda Wischmeyer et al., 157–88. Berlin: de Gruyter, 2014.

———. "Ersättningsteologins historiska bakgrund." *Nordisk judaistik* 19 (1998) 89–108.

———. *Förundran och förväntan*. Stockholm: Verbum, 2012.

———. "'Gör detta till min åminnelse': Minne och manipulation i tidiga judisk-kristna relationer." In *Minne och manipulation: Om det kollektiva minnets praktiker*, edited by Barbara Törnquist Plewa and Ingrid Rausch, 35–51. Lund: Centrum för Europaforskning, 2013.

———. "Introduction: 'For Six Strange Weeks They Had Acted as if They Were Friends.'" In *Religious Stereotyping and Interreligious Relations*, edited by Jesper Svartvik and Jakob Wirén, 1–18. New York: Palgrave Macmillan, 2013.

———. "'Jag är Josef, er bror, som ni sålde till Egypten.'" In *Levande ord: Tolkningar av abrahamitiska källtexter*, edited by Susanne Olsson and Hanna Stenström, 61–78. Lund: Studentlitteratur, 2011.

———. "Judisk tro och kristen i ett religionsteologiskt perspektiv." In *Hela jorden är Herrens: Olika tro sida vid sida*, edited by Birger Olsson, 57–70. Lund: Teologiska institutionen, 2001.

———. "Påskaftonstro." In *Påskboken*, 112–14. Stockholm: Verbum, 2012.

———. "Reading the Epistle to the Hebrews without Presupposing Supersessionism." In *Christ Jesus and the Jewish People Today: New Explorations of Theological Interrelationships*, edited by Philip A. Cunningham et al., 77–91. Grand Rapids: Eerdmans, 2011.

———. "Rendering the Rending of the Veil: What Difference Does It Make?" In *Making a Difference: Essays on the Bible and Judaism in Honor of Tamara Cohn Eskenazi*, edited by David J. A. Clines et al., 257–76. Sheffield, UK: Sheffield Phoenix, 2012.

———. *Skriftens ansikten: Konsten att läsa mellan raderna*. 2nd ed. Lund: Arcus, 2005.

———. *Textens tilltal: Konsten att bilda meningar*. Lund: Arcus, 2009.

Svensk Teologisk Kvartalskrift 86.4 (2010).

Swaim, Lawrence, "The Death of Christianity." *Tikkun* 27.4 (2012) 20–27.

Talmud Bavli: 'im kol ha-mepharshim. 20 vols. Jerusalem: Ha-Talmud ha-mephoar, 1973.

Taylor, Miriam S. *Anti-Judaism and Early Christian Identity: A Critique of the Scholarly Consensus*. Leiden: Brill, 1995.

Terrell, JoAnn M. "What Manner of Love?" In *The Passion of the Lord: African American Reflections*, edited by James A. Noel and Matthew V. Johnson, 51–76. Minneapolis: Fortress, 2005.

Thiselton, Anthony C. *Hermeneutics: An Introduction*. Grand Rapids: Eerdmans, 2009.

Thunberg, Lars. *Den gudomliga ekonomin: Fornkyrkliga perspektiv*. Skellefteå: Artos, 2001.

Tyson, Joseph B. "The Death of Jesus." In *Seeing Judaism Anew: Christianity's Sacred Obligation*, edited by Mary C. Boys, 38–45. Lanham, MD: Rowman & Littlefield, 2005.

Ullucci, Daniel C. *The Christian Rejection of Animal Sacrifice*. Oxford: Oxford University Press, 2012.

———. "Contesting the Meaning of Animal Sacrifice." In *Ancient Mediterranean Sacrifice*, edited by Jennifer Wright and Zsuzsanna Várhelyi, 57–74. Oxford: Oxford University Press, 2011.

Vallgren, Carl-Johan. *Den vidunderliga kärlekens historia*. Stockholm: MånPocket, 2002.

Volf, Miroslav. *The End of Memory: Remembering Rightly in a Violent World*. Grand Rapids: Eerdmans, 2006.

Wainwright, Geoffrey. "Eucharist." In *Oxford Companion to Christian Thought*, edited by Adrian Hastings et al., 214–17. Oxford: Oxford University Press, 2000.

Wallace, W. Jason. *Catholics, Slaveholders, and the Dilemma of American Evangelicalism, 1835–1860*. Notre Dame, IN: University of Notre Dame Press, 2010.

Washington, James Melvin, ed. *A Testament of Hope: The Essential Writings and Speeches of Martin Luther King, Jr.* San Francisco: Harper San Francisco, 1986.

Weedman, Gary E. "Reading Ephesians from the New Perspective on Paul." *Leaven* 14.2 (2006) 81–92.

Werblowsky, J. Zwi, and C. Jouco Bleeker, eds. *Types of Redemption: Contributions to the Theme of the Study-Conference Held at Jerusalem 14th to 19th July 1968*. Leiden: Brill, 1970.

Werner, Erik. "Melito of Sardis: The First Poet of Deicide." *Hebrew Union College Annual* 37 (1966) 191–210.

Wessén, Elias. *Våra ord: Deras uttal och ursprung*. 2nd ed. Stockholm: Norstedts, 1960.

Whybray, Norman. *Job*. Sheffield, UK: Sheffield Phoenix, 2008.

Wijk-Bos, Johanna W. H. van. "Writing on the Water: The Ineffable Name of God." In *Jews, Christians, and the Theology of the Hebrew Scriptures*, edited by Alice Ogden Bellis, and Joel S. Kaminsky, 45–59. Atlanta: Society of Biblical Literature, 2000.

Williams, Demetrius K. "Identifying with the Cross of Christ." In *The Passion of the Lord: African American Reflections*, edited by James A. Noel, and Matthew V. Johnson, 77–110. Minneapolis: Fortress, 2005.

Williams, Rowan. *Resurrection: Interpreting the Easter Gospel*. 2nd ed. London: Darton, Longman & Todd, 2002.

Williamson, Clark M., and Ronald J. Allen. *Interpreting Difficult Texts: Anti-Judaism and Christian Preaching*. London: SCM, 1989.

Willmer, Haddon. "Forgiveness." In *Oxford Companion to Christian Thought*, edited by Adrian Hastings et al., 245–47. Oxford: Oxford University Press, 2000.

Wolfers, David. *Deep Things out of Darkness: The Book of Job. Essays and a New English Translation*. Grand Rapids: Eerdmans, 1995.

Wright, N. T. *The New Testament and the People of God*. London: SPCK, 1992.

Yee, Tet-Lim N. *Jews, Gentiles and Ethnic Reconciliation: Paul's Jewish Identity and Ephesians*. Cambridge: Cambridge University Press, 2005.

Zlotowitz, Meir, and Nosson Scherman. *Bereishis: Genesis. A New Translation with a Commentary Anthologized from Talmudic, Midrashic and Rabbinic Sources*. 2 vols. 2nd ed. Brooklyn: Mesorah, 1986.

———. *Koheles: Ecclesiastes. A New Translation with a Commentary Anthologized from Talmudic, Midrashic and Rabbinic Sources*. 2nd ed. Brooklyn, NY: Mesorah, 1977.

Index